MW01098585

HOUSEPLANT
OASIS

A GUIDE TO
CARING FOR YOUR PLANTS
+ STYLING THEM IN YOUR HOME

MELISSA LO

PAGE STREET
PUBLISHING CO.

PAGE STREET
PUBLISHING CO.

Copyright © 2022 Melissa Lo

First published in 2022 by
Page Street Publishing Co.
27 Congress Street, Suite 1511
Salem, MA 01970
www.pagestreetpublishing.com

All rights reserved. No part of this book may be reproduced or used, in any form or by any means, electronic or mechanical, without prior permission in writing from the publisher.

Distributed by Macmillan, sales in Canada by The Canadian Manda Group.

26   25   24   23   22   1   2   3   4   5

ISBN-13: 978-1-64567-506-8
ISBN-10: 1-64567-506-8

Library of Congress Control Number: 2021938429

Cover design by Melissa Lo and book design by Kylie Alexander for Page Street Publishing Co. Photography by Melissa Lo, with contributions from Justin Wong and Danielle Sum. Photographs of pests on pages 63, 64 and 67 by Koppert Biological Systems.

Printed and bound in The United States

Page Street Publishing protects our planet by donating to nonprofits like The Trustees, which focuses on local land conservation.

TO RONAN + KALI:

Drink plenty of water,
Get lots of sunshine.
Reach high to the sky,
But stay grounded.
Go out on a limb,
Bend before you break.

Always keep growing.

TABLE OF CONTENTS

INTRODUCTION

As humans, we are wired with a natural affinity to nature and living things. Being in and around nature has a mood-boosting and calming effect. Perhaps it is the crisp morning air that fills your nostrils and hits your lungs during a morning hike through a wooded trail, a time when you find yourself lost in the intricate lattice of a single snowflake, the experience of looking up high at the billowing soft cloud formations painted across a sunset sky or the feeling of the millions of tiny grains of sand that envelop your feet as soon as you take your shoes off at a sandy beach. It is in these small but significant moments that we develop our appreciation for the finite earthly treasures that we've evolved to take for granted.

Surrounding yourself with plants can ease your state of mind and help reduce stress, anxiety and negativity, making room to increase motivation, productivity and creativity. Because plants can't speak, it takes a certain amount of obser-vation and awareness to keep them happy and thriving. The very act of tending houseplants puts me in a state of consciousness and grounds me in the moment to nurture them for the future. The process has a calming and meditative effect, and watching them thrive and evolve is deeply gratifying.

Take a journey into the world of plant parenthood and embrace not just the aesthetic aspects of houseplants, but also the benefits and enjoyment caring for them can offer. Learn about the minutiae of plant care principles and how the smallest of nuances can affect their growth. Watch them take shape in response to light, growing mediums, nutrients, temperature and even the types of water that you provide as the ultimate caregiver of their livelihood.

There is a plant to suit each individual on the varying plant parenting spectrum, and taking the time to learn which ones complement your lifestyle and décor sense is all part of the journey and fun. Immerse yourself in the plethora of plant species and cultivars and watch your collection grow with each green baby you acquire. Explore the different ways to display houseplants in a space to seamlessly and beautifully enhance the ambiance of your home.

I hope that by the end of this book, you will develop the basic tools and knowledge to slow life down just a bit, hone your senses and appreciate the beauty, benefits and complexities of houseplants. Get inspired to make green-ery a part of your daily refuge and ultimately to rekindle and reconnect yourself to nature in your own individual oasis.

ACQUISITION

BRINGING THE OUTDOORS IN

There is a cornucopia of plant dealers to whet the appetite of every type of plant parent—for the busy absentee plant parent who enjoys the look of plants, but doesn't want the full-time commitment; the experimental plant parent looking to try all the houseplants, and grow methods and track their progress over time; the scrupulous plant parent in pursuit of the next coveted trendy cultivar; and every type in between.

Whatever the stage, phase or level of expertise, houseplant acquisition is a fun and exciting process that marks a milestone in plant parenthood. If you're just starting out, arm yourself with the knowledge of The Principles of Care outlined on pages 21 to 85 and begin with a few green babies to see how they align with your lifestyle and commitment level. Many of the plants highlighted in the Hero Houseplants chapter (page 87) are recommended for beginners, so select a few that pique your fancy and grow your green family from there.

The popularity and love for houseplants that have exploded in recent times have made acquiring houseplants easier than ever, making them readily available in every possible retail outlet. There's an experience for every type of shopper, so don't limit yourself to just one source—diversify your green collection by visiting my recommendations.

Valleyview Gardens, a garden center located in Ontario, Canada, is open year round offering a diverse collection of plants and products.

HOW TO FIND YOUR NEXT GREEN GEM

Nurseries + Garden Centers

As my number one go-to, these large establishments will sell plants of many species and cultivars of varying sizes and formats year round. Find all of your specialty houseplant needs in these stores—stakes, substrates, pest control products and more. The staff are there to help if you have specific product or care questions. Because the many options available can be somewhat overwhelming, looking for care cards with tips on lighting requirements, bringing a wish list, conducting some quick research on your phone or starting with a smaller-sized plant can all alleviate the stress of the selection process. Stroll through lush rows of healthy potted specimens, soak up the oxygenated air and feast your eyes on the bounty of greens.

Big Box Retailers

Large retail chains such as Home Depot, Walmart, IKEA or Costco purchase a selection of plants in mass volume from wholesalers, sometimes offering a slight discount compared to other plant dealers. These outlets are convenient if you're looking for a quick one-stop shopping experience to coincide with your grocery run, but expect limited choices with availability only during the growing or gardening seasons such as the spring and summer months. Because plants sold here are not as closely monitored and cared for by staff, thoroughly observe the health and conditions of the specimens and avoid purchasing plants that appear to be waterlogged and have root rot or have any obvious signs of disease or pests.

Local Retailers

Your neighborhood convenience and grocery stores, floral or plant boutiques, farmers' and flea markets and special event pop-ups are many of the smaller-scale businesses worth perusing for your next leafy gem. These retailers stock a selection of plants in small handpicked batches where you might very well find the perfect little specimen calling for you to bring it home. If you have something specific in mind, these local plant shops can sometimes accommodate and help you check off your wish list by sourcing and ordering by request. Get your foliage fix and support your local community by visiting your neighborhood plant dealers.

Friends, Family + Community

Sometimes you can find plants available right under your nose. Cuttings shared by friends and family is a fun and easy way of acquiring plants free of charge—with expert advice at your fingertips from people who have already cared for the same plant. In a similar vein, keep an eye on local listings or message boards for cuttings or previously owned plants in search of new homes whilst conducting a thorough background check on their current health and the conditions they were grown in. Enlist yourself for the next organized community plant swap or join the growing online community for tips, tricks and discussions on plant care with like-minded enthusiasts.

Online

Armed with a smart device and in your favorite pajamas, shop for plants in the comfort of your own home from online retailers such as Amazon, Etsy, eBay and independently owned e-commerce businesses, to name just a few. You're just a couple of keywords and several clicks away from a visual plethora of plants varying in origins, formats, conditions and price tags—from the run-of-the-mill to the rarest-of-rare, delivered right to your doorstep. Although online shopping has become a highly convenient and widely utilized method of acquiring plants, what you see in the photo advertised is not always what you will get in the mail. Do your research, use reputable suppliers and be wary of over- and under-priced specimens or obscure suppliers—there is potential for bringing unwanted pests and diseases into the home, as well as invasive species or damaged or dead specimens with no guarantee or return policy.

CHOOSING PLANTS

How do you make houseplant acquisition a fun and less intimidating process? Before you take out your wallet, ask yourself the following questions:

Where will this plant live in my home and what kind—amount and intensity—of light will it receive?

What types of qualities or considerations does this plant require?

How much time can I afford to care for this plant based on my current schedule and lifestyle?

The first and foremost factor before selecting a plant is determining the availability of light in the proposed area of your home. Ensuring an adequate amount and intensity of light for any given plant will give the best start to a newly acquired specimen and ensure its health and longevity under your care. First, locate the window or windows relative to the spot you want to position your plant and determine the direction and intensity throughout the day in which natural light enters through these light sources. In short, a south-facing window will give you the longest duration with varying intensities throughout the day, east-facing emitting several hours of soft morning light, west-facing several hours of warmer afternoon light and the lowest level and intensity of light coming from north-facing windows year round. See page 23 for more on light.

The houseplant selection process can sometimes be circumstantial and based on a specific need or situation. Perhaps you are searching for nontoxic plants that are safe to grow around pets and children; you want to create a privacy screen between two areas of the home; you want to create vertical interest in an open space with tall ceilings or require something compact and slow growing for smaller spaces. Aligning your plant choices with your specific living situation can help with the selection process.

Assess your current lifestyle and determine how much time you want to commit to caring for houseplants. Review The Principles of Care covered on pages 21 to 85 to get a sense of the maintenance and all of the various factors involved with plant parenthood. Plant ownership should enhance your well-being, complement your lifestyle and exist in harmony in the home environment. There is a plant for every type of plant parent. At the least, expect to water a single plant once a month, while some individuals may find joy in daily misting, pruning and monitoring of potential pest activity for a number of plants.

Once you have a plant in mind to bring home and you have located it from a plant dealer, pick up the plant you want and do a basic assessment to ensure you are selecting the healthiest possible specimen. Look closely and examine the foliage for signs of stress, infestation and disease—the leaves and stems should be firm, erect and vibrant in color and the soil should be free from mold or the presence of questionable insects. If possible, take a look at the roots and make sure they are firm and abundant, white to tan in color, are not overly pot-bound or growing out of the drainage holes.

PLANT PARENTING TIP

The moment you witness new growth from a newly acquired plant is an exciting one—celebrate with a happy dance as your efforts have paid off and your green baby appears to be thriving. Take note of your habits and be consistent, observing any changes and adjusting your care as needed. If you are happy with the level of commitment and outcome of the particular plant, the same care and attention can then be applied to similar species under the same genus, thereby expanding your collection. Level up by exploring different genera of varying species and cultivars as they align with your lifestyle and growing interest.

ADAPTATION PERIOD

There is an adjustment period plants may experience when introduced into a new environment. For instance, immediately moving a specimen that was once growing in a consistently warm, humid and very brightly lit greenhouse into the average household with lower levels of the mentioned environmental factors may throw off the equilibrium of your new acquisition. An initially happy and healthy plant may show some signs of droop or curled leaves, slowed growth, etiolation, yellowing or dropping foliage.

To the best of your ability, try to limit shock by replicating the conditions in which the plant was grown in or learn about the native environment they originated from to get an idea of how they will thrive best. If you are in doubt on what your new plant baby enjoys best, a temporary spot to place them in is a consistently warm and bright, indirectly lit area, free from direct sun or cold drafts. Research its needs and observe its growth closely for the next several weeks and adjust your plant parenting habits accordingly. You can read more about the specific needs of the featured Hero Houseplants on pages 87 to 166.

Though it may be tempting to immediately water and repot your new plant baby once you bring it home, you will sometimes find that the soil is already fully saturated, especially when it has been acquired from nurseries and garden centers aligned with the demands of greenhouse conditions. Repotting may not be necessary if the specimen is coming from a reputable source that has ensured a proper growing medium in an appropriately sized container for the plant to grow into for the next six to twelve months or more.

The adaptation period will vary in duration, and the severity of superficial changes will be based on the type of plant and their adaptability to the new environment in alignment with your attention and commitment to care. Don't be alarmed if you encounter some initial adaptation shock, or if you kill your newly acquired plant. Every plant that dies under your care is an opportunity to improve your habits and methods and to learn about its needs—and of course, an excuse to go to the plant store to acquire new green babies.

THE PRINCIPLE
DESIGN AND C

The principles of design are rules that designers use in combir
visual that is effective and aesthetically pleasing. Typically us
design world, these principles and their relationship between
together to create a sense of harmony and cohesiveness.

As a designer, I practice and apply these principles when sty
home. I've found so much joy in being inspired by nature and ir
of the earth and bringing them right into my living spaces.
have become an everyday part of life and have developed
personal style and taste as I continue to transform every no
green retreat.

Implementing these principles will help to separate a uniq
design versus ordinary or arbitrary placements. Use one, se
principles as you see fit, keeping the rules in mind when shop
as you are styling the home. Below are my top ten design prir
your green spaces and creating eye-catching vignettes.

TOP TEN DESIGN RULES

1. Hierarchy

Also known as *emphasis* or *focal point*, *hierarchy* implies importance in a visual arrangement. When combining plants in a group, rank each by their characteristic feature in descending order with your focal point having the highest ranking. Hierarchy can be reinforced through contrast in proximity, size, color, texture and shape.

2. Texture

Texture describes the surface quality by appearance, feel or consistency of an element or object. Bring compositions to life and put them in context by introducing or highlighting textures with plants and surrounding décor. Textures can be found on the leaves and other parts of a plant, created by the plant as a whole along with the containers they are placed into.

3. Shape

Shape is defined by the form or outline of an element. For houseplants, this could be the shape of a leaf combined with other parts of the plant or an entire silhouette of a specimen, including the container it is housed in. The irregular lines of plants can help soften a look and give an organic feel to a space. Enhance these natural curves by introducing natural fibers, wooden and stone elements into spaces.

4. White Space

Also known as *negative space*, *white space* consists of the areas of a visual that do not contain any elements. These are the areas that are essentially empty which can help to frame and highlight a group of plants or a vignette by increasing visibility and emphasis. Not only should you always leave breathing room for your plants to grow into, but allowing for white space helps direct focus and attention to areas of interest in an elegantly organized way.

5. Contrast

Contrast refers to the juxtaposition between two opposing elements. These differences or opposites help create interest, impact and emphasis in a visual. Contrast in plants can be achieved by juxtaposition in color, texture, shape, size or the containers they are housed in, as well as parts of a plant or its whole.

6. Repetition

Also known as *rhythm* or *similarity,* repetition uses the same or similar elements in design. Using this principle helps to create unity, consistency and cohesiveness. Repetition is not only limited to the use of the same or similar plants, but can also be applied to the planters they are housed in.

7. Variety

Adding contrasting elements can help diversify a vignette and create visual interest. Combine different species of plants with varying colors, sizes, shapes and textures to create the complexity and dynamics to achieve *variety*. Variety can also be achieved with the addition of inanimate objects such as keepsakes, souvenirs or other items of personal interest.

8. Grouping

The relationship between objects can be emphasized when placed in a group, allowing the viewer to draw connections between similar elements. *Grouping* related varieties of plants from the same genus, by growth habits or even a combination of similar planters—cacti in cement planters, ferns in a collection of glass terrariums, pothos in matte black planters—are examples of creating visually cohesive vignettes.

9. Simplicity

The principle of *simplicity* is the discipline of reducing, refining and editing a design to create the most impact. Sometimes less is more. Try removing one, two or even a few elements in a vignette and take a step back to see how it affects the overall composition of a vignette.

10. Movement

Movement describes the path that is created to help the viewer's eye scan from one element to the next. This can be achieved by the direction created through lines, shapes, color and edges of plants and the containers they are put in. As an example, create movement in a vignette by staggering trailing plants on a shelf to lead the eye from the top left corner to the bottom right, as we are naturally trained to read a page.

THE PRINCIPLES OF CARE

Whether you are a new plant parent welcoming their first green baby into the home or a seasoned one adding a new species to their collection, we all have an innate moral obligation or a sense of duty to keep these living things alive. I go through numerous plants in order to find the ones that suit my current lifestyle and continue to do so with my evolving schedules, interest or even moods.

Each plant, even within the same genus, will respond differently to the care you give them. Because we are bringing them into a controlled environment, our homes, we have the ultimate power over the outcome of their well-being and development. The principles of care in this chapter are ordered by importance, so bear this in mind the next time you encounter a problem with your once-thriving plant that has begun to show signs of distress. Go through each section to see if your plant is lacking or receiving too much of something. Being realistic with growth, savoring the process and appreciating the minor imperfections will help alleviate any stress that may arise with plant parenthood.

With the tools and knowledge laid out in the following chapter, you will observe and learn about the needs of your plant babies and adjust each care principle accordingly to see how they respond. The key is being flexible with your routine and tweaking your methods as needed—don't be afraid to get your hands dirty or try a new method to see the change you want.

Remember: Seek progress, not perfection.

LIGHT

When it comes to the factors a plant needs in order to thrive, light remains the most important above everything else. Starve a plant of light and you will soon notice a once happy specimen begin to lose its color, luster, growth and familiar form, resulting in pale or dropping leaves and stunted growth. Notice if a plant is leaning towards a particular direction in response to light—a phenomenon known as phototropism. It may be stretching in search of a brighter light source, resulting in etiolated growth (read more about that on page 59).

Plants use energy from light combined with water and carbon dioxide to produce sugars and oxygen, a process known as photosynthesis. Over time, dust and debris can accumulate on leaf surfaces blocking pores and hindering this process. As part of your general maintenance regimen, include "leaf cleansing" in your routine. For broad-leaved plants, a simple wipe down with a damp soft cloth would suffice, avoiding the use of leaf shine products. These products, often containing mineral oil or wax as the main ingredient, can hinder photosynthesis by reflecting light and blocking transpiration—at worst, this will interfere with the development and survival of the plant.

Better yet, give your green friends the full spa treatment by transferring them into the sink, shower or bathtub and rinse the foliage with room temperature to tepid water—never too cold or hot to avoid shocking your plants. Using a handheld shower attachment is ideal, making sure to spray the undersides and crevices where pests love to hide. Schedule this on watering days to avoid the risk of overwatering. See page 27 to read more on watering your plants.

PLANT PARENTING TIP

Most houseplants fall into the bright but indirect light category. Variegated species require higher levels of light to photosynthesize, due to their reduced amount of chlorophyll. If you suspect a plant is not receiving adequate amounts of light, move it to a brighter spot gradually. Acclimating it in several areas by increasing light levels before positioning it in its final destination will alleviate shock caused by sudden changes in the environment.

We oftentimes come across labels such as "low light tolerable," but what does this exactly mean? It is important to know that plants identified in this category do not thrive in the dark, for example a windowless bathroom, and to recognize that "low" is actually a considerable amount of light—think a few feet removed from a north-facing window as an example. Some plants may tolerate or survive lower light levels, but note that their growth will be slowed or stunted.

When talking about light for plants, the spectrum can be categorized from low to medium to high. The distance from which a plant sits from the light source—even within a foot (30 cm)—will decrease the amount and intensity of light and affect the way it develops. As a general rule of thumb, north- and east-facing windows generate amounts of light that are gentle enough for plants to be placed right beside this light source, while distances beyond this window may begin to stunt the growth of some plants. For south- and west-facing windows, where longer periods and higher intensities of light are generated, you have a range of distances to place plants from high light and heat-loving cacti (page 93) and succulents placed right up on the sills, to ficus trees (page 109), monsteras (page 121) and radiator plants (page 145) that will appreciate gentler indirect light several feet removed from this window and even further in distance, low light tolerant dwellers like snake plants (page 153), pothos (page 141), ZZ plants (page 165) and philodendrons (page 137).

When it comes to the duration of natural light, south-facing windows will produce the most daylight hours, with east-facing windows emitting several comfortable hours of morning light, west-facing windows several hours of the most intense afternoon light and indirect, or low light, coming from northern-facing windows throughout the day. Low light can also be thought of as the amount of light understory plants receive—that is, dappled light shining through the canopy of taller plants. In the home, this can be mimicked by shutters or blinds.

Low light can be thought of as ambient light produced by a small source with no direct sunlight. If you place a plant in this area at noon when the sun is highest, the shadow it casts against a wall would most likely be nonexistent or very faint and it would not see the sky from its position relative to a window. North-facing windows or a room with a window obstructed by another building would produce low light levels. Since this direction will generate the softest intensity of light, I would suggest placing only low light tolerant plants directly in front of this type of light source.

Medium light can be described as partial, filtered, dappled or indirect sunlight generated from a bright light source with gentle direct sunlight. A plant in these areas will cast a soft shadow against a wall and see some of the sky from its position. Partial light is direct sunlight for several hours in the day; east-facing windows, which receive direct light in the morning and west-facing windows, which receive direct afternoon sun, are the best examples of this situation. Filtered light is a consistent amount of light received through a semi sheer layer like that of curtains. Indirect light can be found in the shaded areas adjacent to a consistently bright window.

High light levels are known to be direct sunlight, with consistent sun exposure throughout the day. Plants placed in this range will cast a defined shadow against a wall and see a clear view of the sky. South-facing windows will provide the longest duration of high light exposure, followed by west and east. Keep in mind that intense, direct sun can burn most plants. Seasonal changes can intensify this effect with the rise in summer temperatures. This is especially so in the case of plants placed in west-facing windows where the afternoon heat combined with the sun may become too intense for some plants. Watch for signs of burn marks, crispy leaf margins or bleached foliage.

PLANT PARENTING TIP

Routinely rotate your plants for even growth. When plants are placed in an area with one directional light source, they will tend to veer and grow towards that source—observe the amount of movement for individual plants, as they vary between species and rotate each one as needed.

Front view of leaves growing in the same direction as one light source.

Back view of the same plant as a result of absence in pot rotation.

WATER

Next to light, water is the second most important element in the livelihood of houseplants. But even something as simple as water can affect the outcome of plant growth. Differences in the types, frequency, amount and temperature of water are small variables that you can control to ensure your plant babies are getting the proper hydration they need to thrive.

Before we dive into the nuances of H_2O, let's clarify what the infamous "water thoroughly but don't overwater" phrase means. Overwatering is used to describe a plant—specifically, the root ball—that has drowned in water by remaining too wet, and the roots have now been robbed of oxygen. Within a short period of time, fungal disease develops, attacking the roots and rendering them to mush. Overwatering is a silent killer because more often than not, a plant that has suffered from overwatering is so far into the deep end that there is no chance of recovery, making this the number one cause of plant death. The key to preventing overwatering is to water the plant just enough so that the root ball has access to the moisture it needs and is able to use up and not more. Finding this threshold takes a little patience, practice and perseverance.

Types of Water

"Why can't I just use tap water," you ask? You can certainly use the water provided from the taps of your homes and plants will still grow. However, tap water typically contains chemicals like chlorine, magnesium and fluoride that some plants are especially sensitive to. For example, spider plants (page 157), peace lilies (page 133) and corn plants (page 97) will show browning tips when watered with fluoridated water.

Over time, repeated use of tap water will cause mineral buildup in the soil, wreaking havoc on pH levels. Houseplants generally enjoy a slightly acidic environment of pH levels 6.0 to 7.0. You can alleviate problems with buildup by flushing the soil with running water or adding a few drops of vinegar to the water if you suspect the water to have high pH levels. If you want to be precise, using test strips—available at your local hardware, pet or aquarium supply store and through online retailers like Amazon or eBay—will give you a better reading.

For convenience, I like to have a pitcher of filtered water—like a Brita pitcher with replaceable carbon filters—filled at all times, so that I can quickly top off my plants when they are thirsty. Filtered water is free from chlorine and metals like lead and mercury. If time allows, I will also stockpile this filtered water into 1-gallon (4-L) jugs that I can then add water-soluble supplements like liquid fertilizer, soil enhancers or even hydrogen peroxide to treat pest larvae or mold in the substrate—see page 66 for more on this.

If tap water is your only option for your green babies, leaving it sitting overnight can help dissipate most of the chlorine. Other types of water suitable for watering are spring, rain or melted snow, aquarium, distilled or reverse osmosis water. Spring, rain and aquarium water are all very good options as these are free from harmful chemicals and contain trace minerals that are beneficial to plants.

Still, there are some more types of water that are less than ideal for use. For those who have access to a well, groundwater can vary due to leaching of chemicals from human activity such as fertilizer, as well as natural soil and underground features that can affect the quality of the water drawn. Distilled or reverse osmosis water has been treated to remove bacteria and dissolved beneficial solids and although it can be used for plants, the drawbacks are increased due to the absence of nutrients. Do not use mineral water or water from a soft water system—these contain detectable amounts of additives that are inappropriate for plant health and repeated use may even eventually kill a plant.

PLANT PARENTING TIP

Use residual water from washing or blanching vegetables, boiling eggs, rinsing rice or soaking beans to water your plants—beneficial trace minerals are released into these types of water and can act as fertilizer. This is an eco-friendly way to reuse nutrient-fortified water that you would otherwise be pouring down the drain. Just remember not to use any cooking water that has added salt or oils, be sure to cool boiling water down to room temperature and water only when needed.

When to Water

Use a customized approach when it comes to establishing the frequency of watering your plants and use ranges you see on nursery labels or online as a general guideline only. The frequency of watering will be governed by many variables including the type of plant, amount of light, season, substrate and container size.

A droopy peace lily telling you it's time for a water.

The same peace lily fully revived after a thorough watering.

Hone your senses to look, listen and feel for when your plant needs a drink. Look at the plant—if it looks droopy, has curled, wrinkled or crispy leaves, it may be telling you that it's time to water. Listen to how gently squeezing the nursery container sounds—if the soil sounds crunchy, it's time to bust out the watering can. Feel the weight of the pot—learn the difference in weight of a dried out pot versus a freshly watered one and take a mental note of the average number of days it takes for the plant to typically dry out and water accordingly.

Knowing where your plant originated from and the environment they natively grow in will give you clues to how much water they require. There are different layers in a rainforest, which is where many of your tropical varieties are found, that will generate varying degrees of moisture. The amount of sunlight afforded to each layer affects a plant's watering needs. Plants found in the darkest layer of the forest floor, also known as the low light varieties—such as nerve plants (page 125), ferns (page 105) and peace lilies (page 133)—thrive best in high humidity and consistently moist soil that never completely dries out.

The next layer up, comprised of dappled light, is called the understory and accommodates plants such as monsteras (page 121), pothos (page 141), philodendrons (page 137) and palms (page 129) that still require consistently moist soil, but can tolerate short periods of drought. Many of the plants suitable for the home can be found in these two mentioned layers. They will require watering every five to ten days.

In the top layer, known as the canopy layer, epiphytes can be found—organisms that grow or attach themselves to other plants and objects for support. With their uniquely evolved roots, plants such as the afore-mentioned monsteras (pages 117 and 121), pothos (page 141) and philodendrons (page 137) as well as airplants consistently obtain more sunlight while drawing nutrients and moisture from the air and may not need water as frequently.

Plants from arid to semi-arid regions—characterized by reduced humidity levels, prolonged periods of drought, consistent sun exposure—and grown in coarsely textured sandy soil structures are home to slow growing cacti (page 93) and succulents. Due to the water-storing capacity of these plants, they do not need constant hydration and saturating the root ball once a month is adequate. As a matter of fact, they are sensitive to overwatering, so avoid root rot by allowing them to thrive on neglect.

As mentioned on page 23 in the light section, plants can benefit from showers to increase humidity, remove dust and debris to enhance photosynthesis as well as blast any pesky insects that may be lurking in the crevices or the underside of leaves. Reserve these showers for your humidity-loving, tropical babies only, and keep plants such as succulents and cacti (page 93) clear from the excess drenching. Always use room to tepid water temperatures—think tropical vacation rain—when showering to prevent shock. Timing this spa treatment on watering days can prevent the risk of overwatering. This can be done as frequently as once a week, especially for the smaller specimens that dry out sooner, to a monthly basis for the bigger pots due to their increased capacity to retain moisture.

PLANT PARENTING TIP

Plants love and can benefit greatly from the humidity of regular showers with a thorough rinsing under the garden hose, running faucet or even in the bathtub or shower using a hand-held attachment. If a shower is not feasible, but you still want to boost humidity, you can try grouping plants together, adding a pebble tray with water underneath a pot, misting regularly or setting up a humidifier nearby. Avoid water damaged leaves or fungal growth by ensuring that there is no pooling of water on leaves for extended periods of time—be sure to shake off excess water or increase the air circulation in the environment by opening a window during milder temperatures or turning on a fan.

How to Water

The function of water for plants is to help with transpiration, a process by which water is absorbed from the roots, moved up and evaporated through the plant parts. During this action, water helps maintain rigidity of the plant's structure and regulates its temperature and absorption of nutrients.

A healthy, robust root structure allows optimal nutrient intake and strong anchorage. The key to attaining this is to water thoroughly and deeply, saturating the entire root ball. Gradually water until you see runoff coming through the drainage holes, pause and water some more. This will ensure that the complex root structures have access to moisture. Shallow watering, that is, providing enough water to only saturate the superficial layer of the soil, will stunt the growth of the roots. The roots' hairs, or those very finely textured lateral extensions from the main roots, are essential for nutrient uptake and if allowed to dry out for too long, these structures will begin to shrink and die back, hindering the plant's capacity to absorb these nutrients.

MY UNIVERSAL WATERING GUIDE

1. Look, listen and feel for the need to water. Use a moisture meter if you need to, which is a device used to measure moisture content in soil. They can be found at garden centers, hardware stores or online from retailers such as Amazon.

2. Ensure that there is a drip-tray, saucer, cache pot or other container for catching runoff from watering. Placing your plant in a sink, bathtub or outdoors works too.

3. Water with a slow and even flow, covering all areas of the soil's surface, until you start to see runoff from the drainage holes. Pause, letting any remaining water to channel through the drainage holes and repeat Step 3.

4. Thirsty tropicals can benefit from absorbing the extra runoff by allowing the plant to soak up the water from the drip-tray for about twenty to thirty minutes. Always remember to discard any remaining water that has not been absorbed after this period.

The "soak and dry" method of watering is the technique that I personally use for most if not all of my plants. This involves thoroughly watering and allowing the soil to dry out completely before the next watering and works well on plants that can tolerate occasional, short or long periods of drought. This method does double-duty and ensures that I avoid the risk of over-watering while helping prevent the incidence of fungus gnats that favor damp environments. I use a moisture meter for the medium to bigger and harder-to-reach pots that I cannot otherwise lift or squeeze to let me know they have dried out.

For plants such as cacti (page 93) or succulents that can go for long periods without water—typically three to four weeks between watering—it is not essential to provide enough water until it comes through the drainage holes, but rather just enough to saturate the first few inches of the soil due to their shallow root structures and ability to hold moisture within the plant parts.

Plants without drainage holes will require a drainage layer on the bottom of the planter— see page 76. Avoid overwatering by using a moisture meter. Insert the probe into several areas of the soil and refrain from watering if the indicator reads "wet." Be cautious of watering if the indicator still reads "moist." Most plants can tolerate and may even benefit from fully dried out soil before another thorough watering. And of course, give your plant baby a well-deserved drink if the indicator reads "dry" during your routine checks. Moisture meters are handy for large planters that cannot be lifted to check water weight.

Plants with compacted soil—think ones with a high percentage of peat moss (page 40) or those that prefer not to have wet stems or leaves, such as cacti (page 93), succulents and plants with foliage that touches the top of the soil—can benefit from "bottom-watering" as shown in the photo below. Place the potted plant with drainage holes on top of a dish of water and allow the root ball to soak up the water like a sponge. Pour more water into the dish as needed, discarding any remaining water that is not absorbed within half an hour.

A moisture meter is a device that can be used to measure moisture content in the soil.

Important Considerations

The size of the container housing the plant is an important consideration on how to water. A watered plant contained in an abundant amount of substrate in a large pot will dry out much slower than the same specimen in a smaller container. Keep in mind that plants enjoy being slightly root-bound, which is when the root ball extends and touches the sides of the pot. Overpotting, or when a specimen is potted in a container that is too large and in an excess amount of substrate, can pose risks for overwatering and less than desirable conditions for growth. See page 71 for more information on this topic.

Other factors affecting your watering schedule include the season and weather forecast. During spring and summer when daylight hours are longer and plants are awake and actively growing, they will need to be hydrated more frequently than in the winter when growth will be slowed as they enter dormancy. To a similar effect, a forecast calling for prolonged periods of sunny clear skies during the week will prompt your plants to kickstart photosynthesis into high gear versus a week of clouds, when your plants may not demand as much water.

Note that some plants do not like to dry out too much, especially for long periods of time. For example, most tropical plants such as ferns (page 105), peace lilies (page 133) and nerve plants (page 125) enjoy consistently moist soil, whereas cacti (page 93) and succulents can go for long periods without water. When in doubt, use a moisture meter to take the guesswork out of when to water. As a general rule of thumb, it is always better to err on the side of caution and lean towards the drier end of the spectrum to start, testing the waters and gradually fine-tuning your technique as you learn about the needs of each plant.

TEMPERATURE

Temperature is one of the more negligible factors affecting plant growth. Luckily for us, many of the houseplants on the market are highly adaptable tropical and subtropical species suited to the average household environment. As a general rule of thumb, if you are comfortable in the current temperature of your home, so are your plant babies!

Because most houseplants are tropical, they fair better in warm temperatures rather than cold. The majority will enjoy average household temperatures ranging from around 70°F to 80°F (21°C to 27°C) during the day and 65°F to 70°F (18°C to 21°C) at night, with some plants like cacti (page 93), succulents and other hardier plants tolerating temperatures below and above these ranges. However, be aware that plants are sensitive to drastic temperature fluctuations, so they may suffer if, for example, you suddenly expose your plants to elevated levels of heat when you turn off the air conditioning after having your home consistently cool all summer. Such changes may be detrimental to vulnerable areas such as new growth and propagations.

Ensure that your plants do not touch the windows and are kept away from heating vents and cold drafts as these areas can create temperature extremes leading to leaf damage. Placing plants in temperatures below 50°F (10°C) risks irreversible leaf damage or a halt in growth, while anything lower than 36°F (2°C) can kill a houseplant. In the same vein, never leave plants in the car or outside in the event of a frost advisory when temperatures are expected to fall below 36°F (2°C) or in scorching hot summer sun and heat.

PLANT PARENTING TIP

Superficial leaf damage caused by extreme temperatures are irreversible. However, if the roots are still salvageable, prune away the damaged parts and allow the plant to recover by placing it in a warm and bright spot away from direct sun. In time, expect a full recovery as it bounces back with new growth.

SUBSTRATES

For healthy, thriving plants, start at the foundation—the roots! Often overlooked, this complex underground layer houses the lifeline of the plant where water, air and nutrients from the soil are taken up by the resourceful little root hairs.

The purpose of substrates or soil is to create a basis for roots to thrive in. The ideal medium should support the plant, anchor its roots, retain moisture, drain excess water, be slightly acidic to neutral in pH, be sterile or at least pathogen and seed free, provide nutrients and allow airflow. This is a lot to consider for something as basic as soil, but understanding the makeup of the mixture can make all the difference between an optimally thriving plant and one that is looking a little lackluster despite following proper watering or light requirements.

Never use gardening soil and use bagged, commercial mixes with discretion. Standard commercial mixes, such as Miracle-Gro® potting soil, should at least be amended with 20 to 30 percent perlite to increase aeration. Basic garden soil is far too dense in structural makeup and lacks the appropriate drainage required for all plants. Furthermore, some commercially bagged substrates that state "soil" in the ingredients may not be sterile, posing a risk of contaminants that can harbor insects, unwanted weed seeds or diseases. For this reason, a soilless mix is preferred for houseplants that contains a combination of one part each of a moisture-retaining base of peat moss or coco peat, followed by a structural compound such as coarse sand, coconut chips or bark and finally, an aerating amendment of perlite or pumice.

You can find the substrates described in this chapter at your local nursery, garden center or hardware store. For the harder to find items like coconut husk, pumice or activated charcoal and even custom pre-mixed soils, try searching online on Amazon or for specialty retailers that deliver. I have been able to hunt down quality sphagnum moss from my local specialty tool store through some online research.

Understanding the use plus the pros and cons of the various types of substrates and ingredients can help you customize your composite mixture to better suit the individual palettes of your plant babies, allowing them to thrive at their optimal capacity. Typically, a mixture of a selection of substrates will create the best growing medium compared to using one medium alone. The following is my guide to the most commonly used soil amendments for houseplants.

PEAT MOSS

Peat moss, or sphagnum peat as it is also called, is a by-product of decomposed peat bogs. It is used as a soil conditioner when mixed with other substrates and for its nutrient and water-retentive capabilities. It is the commonly used ingredient found in commercial potting mixes like Miracle-Gro. Although widely used, there are some emerging concerns about the environmental impact of harvesting peat. Due to its very slow growth rate, taking a millennium to form one cubic meter's worth, it is not considered a renewable resource.

Pros	Cons
Widely available	Lowers pH levels
Excellent water retention	Not very nutrient-rich
Prevents soil compaction	Nonrenewable resource
Sterile medium	

COCONUT HUSK

Coconut husk is the by-product of the fibrous material in between the outer coat and inner shell of the coconut. The pith, or coco peat, is used as a soil conditioner when mixed with other substrates and for its nutrient and water-retentive capabilities. The coarse chips (pictured) or mulch can be used to create air pockets in dense mixes or as a top-dressing for aesthetics and moisture retention. Coconut husk is considered a suitable and sustainable alternative to peat moss.

Pros	Cons
Neutral pH levels	Not very nutrient rich
Good water retention	May contain high salt content; rinse before use
Prevents soil compaction	Typically comes in brick form; soak before use
Slow decomposition	
Antifungal properties	
Renewable resource	
Reusable	
Sterile medium	

BARK

Processed bark is the outer most layer of trees, often fir or pine, hammer-milled into small chips and aged or decomposed. Processed bark mulch is a versatile and widely available substrate that decomposes slowly, improves drainage, increases aerating properties and can be used as a top-dressing. Familiarize yourself with the supplier and source of the wood in making this substrate to avoid undesirable contaminants.

Pros	Cons
Adds weight for large or top-heavy plants	Can harbor fungus and disease as it breaks down
Prevents soil compaction	Does not retrain much moisture
Renewable resource	Decomposes quicker than other similar substrates
Available in various grades	Lowers pH as it decomposes
	Not very nutrient rich

SAND

Horticultural sand, also known as coarse or sharp sand is crushed quartz, granite or sandstone used as an amendment for the purpose of improving drainage in a potting medium. Builder's sand can also be used as a cost-effective substitute if horticultural sand is unavailable. Do not use beach sand or sand from coral and shell fragments as these are high in calcium, raising pH level. Do not use sand sourced from the ocean that will contain a salt content too high for houseplants. Avoid plaster or fine grade sands as these can cause soil compaction.

Pros	Cons
Adds some weight for large or top-heavy plants	Not nutrient retentive
Prevents soil compaction	Does not retrain moisture
Reusable	Nonrenewable resource
Does not decompose	Loses efficacy over time
Available in various grades	
Durable	

PERLITE

Perlite is mined obsidian, a volcanic rock that, when crushed and heated at extreme temperatures, pops and expands like popcorn into a lightweight, white-colored granular substrate. This by-product is highly porous with the ability to retain some moisture, but more importantly, it improves drainage by adding a lofty structure to a mix. Perlite is widely available and versatile as both a soilless mix and starter for plants, making it a convenient amendment choice.

Pros

Sterile medium

Neutral pH levels

Prevents soil compaction

Contains trace minerals

Reusable

Does not decompose

Available in various grades

Can be used on its own for rooting cuttings

Cons

Tendency to float to soil surface

Dust particles a respiratory irritant

Nonrenewable resource

PUMICE

Like perlite, pumice is also a naturally occurring volcanic rock that, when heated at extreme temperatures, will combust into a highly porous granular substrate. Pumice comes in a variety of grades and colors, typically used to top-dress soil, or as an amendment to increase structure and improve aeration. Pumice lasts longer than perlite and is considered a more environmentally friendly option due to its minimal processing procedures.

Pros

Sterile medium

Neutral pH levels

Prevents soil compaction

Contains trace minerals

Reusable

Does not decompose

Available in various grades

Can be used on its own for rooting cuttings

Adds weight for top-heavy plants

Durable compared to perlite

Cons

Dust particles in finer grades can be a respiratory irritant

Expensive option compared to perlite

Not as readily available as perlite

VERMICULITE

Yet another naturally occurring mineral, vermiculite expands to golden-brown, accordion-like strands when exposed to extreme temperatures. Vermiculite is available in various grades and used as an amendment to increase water retention and improve aeration. Vermiculite has similar characteristics compared with perlite. However, this amendment has far superior water-retentive capabilities, making its usage quite different.

Pros

Good water retention

Sterile medium

Neutral pH levels

Prevents soil compaction

Contains trace minerals

Reusable

Does not decompose

Available in various grades

Can be used on its own for rooting cuttings

Cons

May increase incidence of overwatering

Raises pH levels

Nonrenewable resource

WORM CASTINGS

Worm castings, used interchangeably with vermicompost, are the by-product of digested organic waste and act as a bioactive form of soil enhancer that is rich in water-soluble nutrients and beneficial microbes. Worm castings can be looked at as a soil enhancer because it feeds the beneficial microorganisms in the soil, creating a fertile environment for plant growth.

Pros	Cons
Environmentally friendly choice	Consistency and quality highly variable
Prevents soil compaction	Takes time to produce if making at home
Neutral pH levels	Improperly broken down worm castings may develop undesirable odors
Gentle organic fertilizer	Shelf life, heat, light and humidity can affect quality
Promotes healthy microorganisms in soilless mixes	
Promotes water retention	
Increases nutrient absorption	
Can repel pests like aphids and mealy bugs	
Can be made at home	

ACTIVATED CHARCOAL

Activated charcoal, used interchangeably with active carbon, is produced when carbon-rich materials such as bamboo, wood, coconut shells, olive pits or coal are combined with a gas and burned at high temperatures, thereby activating them. The result is a highly porous by-product with the ability to trap impurities.

Pros	Cons
Good water retention	Raises pH levels
Sterile medium	
Prevents soil compaction	
Available in various grades	
Prevents mold and odors in soil	
Slow to decompose	
Renewable resource	

SPHAGNUM MOSS

Sphagnum moss comes from the same plant as sphagnum peat moss. But while peat moss is the decaying matter in the deepest layers of peat bogs, sphagnum moss is the living plant itself, harvested on the surface layer. This fibrous medium can be used exclusively on its own as a starter for cuttings, amended in a mix to increase moisture retention or as a top-dressing for decorative purposes and to reduce evaporation from the soil's surface.

Pros	Cons
Sterile medium	Lowers pH as it decomposes
Neutral pH levels when fresh	May not provide adequate aeration
Excellent water retention	May increase incidence of overwatering
Excellent for top-dressing	Not very nutrient rich
Reusable if clean and not decomposed	Higher in cost
Renewable resource	

COMPOST

Compost is the by-product of organic waste, either vegetative or animal waste, broken down into a homogenous substrate chock-full of nutrients. It is available in bagged form for purchase or you can make your own at home. Compost can be used as the basis of a potting mix, however using it as an amendment in smaller amounts to feed plants is more effective due to the rapid rate of breakdown.

Pros	Cons
Environmentally friendly choice	May contain weed seeds or other contaminants
Gentle organic fertilizer	May harbor unwanted pests and bacteria
Good water retention	Improperly broken-down compost may develop undesirable odors
Nutrient rich	Quick to break down
Neutral pH levels	
Contains beneficial organisms	
Can be made at home	

SOIL MIX RECIPES

Armed with the knowledge on the different kinds of substrates, you can experiment with some mixes catered to the tastes of various plants under your care or try some of my personal recipes below, adjusting proportions as needed:

Tropical Mix

50% peat moss or coco peat
20% coconut husk or bark
20% perlite or pumice
10% worm castings or compost
Handful of activated charcoal (optional)

Cactus + Succulent Mix

33% peat moss or coco peat
33% coarse sand
33% perlite or pumice

Aroid Mix

30% peat moss or coco peat
30% coconut husk or bark
30% perlite or pumice
10% worm castings or compost
Handful of activated charcoal (optional)

Read the labels to determine whether the substrate has added nutrients or fertilizers to help you decide whether or not supplementation is required. See page 54 for additional information on feeding your plants. For the sake of convenience, economy and time, prepackaged potting mixes and soil can suffice, provided that they contain an amendment like perlite for drainage. Again, if you are using common potting soil such as Miracle-Gro, amend with extra perlite. There are different mixes labeled for broad categories of plants such as tropical, cacti and succulent, orchid, etc., commonly available at your local hardware store, garden center and nursery. For the lazy plant parent or if you don't have perlite on hand, cacti and succulent mixes can be used as a substitute to increase drainage in dense substrates.

NUTRIENTS

We all know plants need light, water and air to survive. But nutrients are often overlooked and can make an impact on plant growth and vitality. As mentioned in the light section (page 23), plants produce sugars via photosynthesis for fuel. In addition, macro and micronutrients—think supplements—are absorbed by the roots and are necessary for the metabolic processes of plants.

Houseplants that grow in our homes differ from vegetation grown in the ground outdoors and especially in the wild when it comes to how they acquire nutrients to thrive. In nature, plants have an infinite buffet of nutrients to feast on, through a constant cycle of decaying matter on the forest floor. However, container-grown plants are limited to the resources they are placed in and therefore need your help to replenish depleted nutrients.

Fertilization is commonly recommended during the growing seasons of spring and summer during active growth. However, feeding can become part of your plant parenting routine on an ongoing basis throughout the year if you observe continued growth. This is especially true for hungry and vigorous feeders like monsteras (page 121), palms (page 129), birds of paradise (page 89) and many other broad-leaf or fast-growing tropicals. Reduce the amount and frequency during the cooler months to counteract the effects of shorter daylight hours when plants are growing slower or undergoing their resting period.

It is not uncommon to bring home a plant that has been potted in a soil mixture that includes some kind of fertilizer especially prepared for your new green baby. However, it won't be long before the nutrients become exhausted and your plant starts to lose its luster and vibrancy, has slowed or stunted growth or shows leaves starting to turn yellow and drop. On the opposite end of the spectrum, over-fertilization can also cause distress and is marked by signs of burn on leaf margins and tips, accumulation of salts on the soil's surface, yellowing and wilting of lower leaves and also dropping leaves.

Organic and Chemical Fertilizers

Organic fertilizers, also known as soil conditioners and enhancers, are chemical free or "natural" and available either as an animal by-product or plant-based derivative. Some examples of organic fertilizers include but are not limited to: animal manure, bone meal, fish emulsion, compost and worm castings. Organic fertilizers are slow-release types that require time to decompose by means of beneficial microorganisms in order for the nutrients to become bioavailable, that is, available for absorption.

Chemical fertilizers, also known as inorganic or artificial fertilizers, are synthetically manufactured and have specific ratios of nutrients and chemical fillers. The nutrients in these chemical fertilizers are refined to their pure state and void of substances that break down or control their availability. Chemical fertilizers can be resin-coated to give them a slow-release effect, delivering nutrients each time you water.

Fertilizer Values and What They Mean

Commercial fertilizers are labeled with a breakdown of three macronutrients required by plants and expressed as a ratio.

Nitrogen (N): responsible for the growth of plant structures and promotes the green color in plants

Phosphorus (P): known to help strengthen root, seed, flower and fruit development

Potassium (K): benefits overall plant functions to promote pest and disease resistance

As the word suggests, macronutrients are fed to plants in larger amounts, with the primary nutrients expressed as a ratio broken down into nitrogen, phosphorus and potassium (N-P-K) values. Micronutrients, also vital to plant health, are required in smaller amounts from elements such as iron, copper and zinc, to name a few. The higher the ratio values in N-P-K, the more concentrated than that of the lower ones. As a general rule of thumb, look for balanced fertilizers that contain equal values like 20-20-20 and 10-10-10, for example, and those that include micronutrients. These will give your plant a well-rounded boost of nutrients for overall health and development.

If you are using commercially bagged soil or mixes, read the labels to determine whether they have been amended with fertilizer. If not, it is worthwhile to purchase some to have on hand. Having fertilizers handy in your houseplant arsenal are essential if you are concocting your own mixes. Liquid, powder, granular, stick, pod and capsule formulations are the many various application methods available for purchase.

PLANT PARENTING TIP

Liquid- or water-soluble fertilizers are dissolved with water then applied to plants. This concoction can also be used as a foliar spray, where small amounts of nutrients are entered through the leaves' stomata, that is, pores. Give your plants a spa moment by treating them with a nutrient-rich spritz regularly.

Organic vs Chemical Fertilizers

	ORGANIC FERTILIZER	CHEMICAL FERTILIZER
Cost	More expensive	More cost-effective
Pet and Child-Safe	Yes	No, use with caution
Application Frequency	Infrequent	May require frequent applications
Ease of Application	May take extra effort	Easy and convenient
Environmentally Friendly	Yes, can also be homemade	No, mostly made of nonrenewable resources
Odor	May be off-putting, as some types may not be completely decomposed	Typically odorless
Risk of Fertilizer Burn	Low	Yes, danger of over-fertilization
Toxic Buildup	Little to none	Repeated applications may lead to toxic buildup
Nutrient Ratios	May be unknown or unclear	Analyzed to ensure exact ratio of nutrients
Trace Nutrient Availability	Some trace nutrients, but may not be a complete fertilizer	More likely to provide and list micronutrients
Nutrient Accessibility	Takes some time for plants to access	Immediate access and quick results
Effect on Microbial Activity in Soil	Boosts microbial activity in soil	Does not promote bioactive environments in soil and tends to leach nutrients away from plants
Effect on Soil Structure	Improves soil texture, drainage and aeration	Does not benefit soil structure

With a similar mantra to watering, fertilizing should be done with a light hand and it's always safer to err on the side of caution by reducing the frequency and amount. Always read labels and dilute chemical fertilizers with water by half the amount to start, in order to be on the gentler side of feeding. Incorporating fertilization into your plant care routine can ensure they grow at their optimal levels, helping to ward off pests and diseases while looking their best.

DIAGNOSTICS

As mentioned in the Acquisition chapter (page 9), knowing the conditions of where your plant came from—whether that was its ancestral origin or where it was commercially grown—and what type of substrates it was grown in will offer some foresight into the needs of your new plant. Furthermore, bringing home a healthy plant in an appropriate medium will give you the best start to learning its needs and tolerances. Maintaining a healthy plant will be much easier than trying to revive a sick specimen, although there is quite a fulfillment in successfully recovering a once dying plant.

Don't panic if your once happy plant baby is suddenly showing signs of yellowing leaves, drooping, has developed brown spots or is even riddled with crawling insects. Houseplants are, after all, complex living things that undergo a multitude of metabolic processes, and we can only appreciate their ability to tell us their needs by showing these signs. With every bump on the road experienced by a plant complication, knowledge can be gained to better equip yourself with tackling—and more importantly, preventing—future issues.

There are a multitude of houseplant problems that can occur, throwing off their equilibrium. Though not an exhaustive list and keeping in mind that different types of plants have varying displays of exhibiting stress, the following are some of the commonly experienced plant parenting problems caused by environmental and biological factors and how to diagnose, correct and prevent them.

Drooping or Wilting

A plant with healthy looking leaves that was once firm and upright but is now looking excessively limp may be caused by underwatering. This is especially true when the plant is marked by crisp brown leaves. Drooping can also be a sign of overwatering, which causes leaves to become soft, rapidly yellow and defoliate from the bottom up. If watering amounts are adequate and the plant still exhibits droop, move it to a brighter location. Drooping may also be seen with changes in environment, such as acclimating a new plant into the home, as well as after repotting as a sign of transplant shock. In both of these instances, the plant should recover if given time. A plant that has been in the same substrate for several years may begin to show signs of droop as it may have exhausted the medium. In this case, repot with a fresh mixture, sizing up the pot if necessary. Extreme hot and cold temperatures can also result in wilting plants. Damage caused by high heat or frost is irreversible and is marked by darkened areas and a shriveling of the leaves. Quickly remove the wilting plant from the current environment into an area with appropriate temperatures and light conditions to allow for recovery and refrain from overwatering and fertilizing until the specimen has stabilized.

Drooping or Wilting

Etiolation

Defoliation

Etiolation

Etiolation is caused by insufficient light and is characterized by leggy, weakened stems, small leaves and spindly internodes, the parts of the stem between two nodes where leaves form. Unfortunately, the structural deformity cannot be reversed. Commonly seen with succulents, plant parts can be propagated to produce new plants. Tropicals can slowly be acclimated to brighter locations to mitigate further stretching. To prevent etiolation from occurring, place newly acquired plants in appropriate light conditions.

Defoliation

Bear in mind that gradual leaf turnover is extremely common and expected throughout the lifespan of any plant and not a cause of concern. However, there are many reasons for leaves to rapidly defoliate, typically beginning from the lower areas of the plant, as this is a defense mechanism for dealing with extreme shock. Excessive overwatering, underwatering, transplantation, rapid changes in environment, nutrient deficiencies and over-fertilizing are causes of immoderate leaf drop. Correct the issue by first reassessing your watering habits and the plant's current lighting conditions and adjust appropriately. Prevent severe leaf drop by limiting exposure to extreme changes in environment, avoiding immediate repotting, limiting excessive pruning and fertilizing only when required.

Brown Tips

The major causes of browning on the tips of foliage are due to improper fertilization, the type of water used or inadequate humidity. See the photo on page 56. Some species like spider plants (page 157), peace lilies (page 133) and corn plants (page 97) are especially sensitive to fluoride most commonly found in tap water. Flush the soil of your plants with water seasonally to leach salt buildup. Alternatively, scrape away affected areas which appear as a crusty white layer on the soil's surface and then top-dress or repot entirely with fresh substrate. More so an aesthetic setback than a cause for major concern, brown tips can be easily removed using sharp, clean scissors while preserving the shape of the individual leaves by cutting on an angle if possible. Prevent irreversible tip burn by increasing humidity, using filtered, rain or aquarium water and feeding with organic or limited amounts of chemical fertilizers.

Yellowing Leaves

There are a number of reasons your foliage might turn yellow. To reiterate, it is completely normal to experience gradual leaf turnover. It is the combination of rapid yellowing paired with other anatomical abnormalities that can clue you into what the underlying issue may be. Yellowing combined with the wilting of leaves that spread from the bottom up could be a sign of overwatering. Continuous exposure to waterlogged soil, blackened stems and fungus gnats are tell-tale signs of root rot. Refer to the root rot section on page 68 if you suspect a plant is overwatered and how to remedy the situation. Conversely, a thirsty plant may show signs of drooping and curling leaves, followed by yellowing and finally turning crispy brown. Prevent damage due to dehydration by watering thoroughly and consistently. Too much light can lead to yellowing of leaves, causing a sun-bleached effect, making the leaves pale. Extreme intensities of light involving direct sun can further leave burn marks. Reduce the intensity of light exposure by screening with a filter like curtains, blinds or other plants. Even pulling the plant back slightly from the light source can make a big difference in the intensity of light.

Fertilizer Burn

A lack in nutrients can also cause stunted growth, color loss or change in the coloration of leaves commonly shown in new and old growth. On the other hand, an excess of nutrients (or over-fertilization) causes yellowing of leaves with browning margins. Bear in mind, the newly acquired plants you bring home may very likely already have fertilizer—either a slow- or quick-release granular feed—amended into the soil, so avoid excess feeding. Flush plants with running water seasonally to leach excess salt buildup and reduce the amounts and frequency of feeding. Always read the usage labels on fertilizers and practice diluting with water, by half the recommended amounts to avoid over-fertilization. Alternatively, use organic fertilizers, which are gentler and likely won't burn your plants.

Yellowing Leaves

Leaf Scorch

Leaf Scorch

We know plants need sunlight to thrive, but too much of a good thing can lead to sunburn. Some plants may exhibit initial yellowing before brown marks or patches develop. Immediate placement of a plant in direct sunlight for prolonged periods can surely scorch the leaves of a plant that had settled in a less intense location. If you suspect a plant requires higher light levels and needs to be relocated, do so gradually by introducing increasing levels of intensity incrementally over the course of several weeks. This also allows you to observe how they perform with these subtle environmental adjustments. Avoid shock by limiting extreme environmental fluctuations and prevent leaf scorch by using a filter to dampen the intensity of direct sunlight.

PESTS

Houseplant pests are synonymous with plant parenthood. With a myriad of pest types, each unique in their motility, feeding behavior, breeding habit and levels of destruction, there is never a shortage of pesky bugs to keep every plant parent on their toes and on high alert for the next possible attack. From the irritating feeble-flying fungus gnat to the creepy-crawly microscopic spider mite to the ruthless crop-sucking thrips, we can all agree that discovering an infestation really throws a wrench in what is supposed to be a peaceful and relaxing hobby.

Without nature's rain, changing of seasons and natural predators to control pest populations, it is up to you to closely monitor, identify and take appropriate measures to battle these unwelcomed guests. Don't falter if you come across an infestation—try various techniques described below, be patient and above all, be relentless in your fight!

All of the insecticides and biological control methods described below are mild and safe to use in the household and around children and pets. Identify, salvage and prevent future outbreaks with the following commonly experienced houseplant pests:

Fungus Gnats

A common houseplant pest that closely resembles fruit flies and are often mistaken as such, fungus gnats are more of a nuisance than a large threat to the livelihood of a plant. These erratic and weak fliers breed around moist and humid environments, feeding on fungal growth. For minor infestations, use a two-pronged approach for eradicating multiple growth cycles of gnats. Use yellow sticky traps, placed just above the soil's surface to trap adults. To target larvae and eggs in the soil, introduce mosquito dunks, which are dry pellets containing beneficial bacteria. You could also try 3 percent hydrogen peroxide at a dilution of 1:20 with your watering schedule for the next few weeks to a month, or until there is a noticeable reduction in numbers. I would recommend a complete repotting of plants that have a severe infestation. To prevent fungus gnats, avoid overwatering, wait for the soil to dry out slightly or completely before watering again, use a sterile soilless mix (see page 39) or amend your potting medium with horticultural charcoal to reduce mold growth and perlite to increase drainage.

Thrips

Notable for their destruction and notorious resilience to many pesticides, thrips are stealthy in their M.O., leaving plants to be diagnosed with an infestation long after the damage has already been done. They are weak-flying slender insects, brown to black in color and measuring only several millimeters in length. Though minute in size and nonconventional in flying, these destructive insects feed on the juices of stems and leaf cells, gradually weakening the plant while branding foliage with silvery to bronze scars and leaving excrements, seen as tiny black specks, wherever they've happily feasted. These generalist feeders do not have discerning palates and in a short amount of time, expect surrounding plants to be affected as well. For mild infestations and smaller specimens, gingerly remove the plant from its planter, discarding the soil that may be contaminated from nymphs (or young thrips) that may be seeking shelter there during development. Fill a small basin of tepid water and soak the plant in a diluted solution of water with about half a teaspoon of mild dish or castile soap and about a quarter-teaspoon of neem oil, gently rubbing all sides of the leaves and removing traces of soil in the roots. Rinse and repot in fresh soil. Follow with weekly treatments of my Homemade Insecticidal Soap Spray (page 66) with the addition of neem oil (read more on page 65).

Fungus gnat

Thrips

Spider mite

Mealybugs

Spider Mites

As a close relative of spiders, spider mites are microscopic in size, measuring less than ½ millimeter in size and are typically off-white to yellow in color, but can vary from red, brown or green depending on the species. A tell-tale sign of a spider mite infestation is marked by their fine silk webbing and pale yellow stippling on foliage from where they have fed. Spider mites thrive in dry and stale environments, especially during the winter. Increasing humidity and air circulation while giving your plants regular inspections, showers and leaf cleansings will all prevent the likelihood of a spider mite infestation.

Mealybugs

Soft-bodied, wingless insects typically found in white cotton-like clusters, mealybugs are sluggish travelers that typically hide out in crevices where leaves join the stem, within areas of new growth and the undersides of leaves, happily feeding on plant juices. Prune light infestations or take a cotton ball or swab dipped in 70 percent isopropyl alcohol to dab and lift the insects. For larger colonies, prune no more than a third of heavily infested plant parts and thoroughly hose or shower down the infected plant. Follow with a diluted alcohol and water solution of 1:5 ratio—or stronger for more robust plants—and spray liberally, covering all leaf surfaces and crevices. Let the solution sit for about fifteen minutes and rinse thoroughly.

SPECIAL TREATMENTS

Neem Oil

Neem oil is a natural, plant-based concentrated oil, extracted from the seeds of neem trees. When used for pest control, the oil acts in several short- and long-term ways to deter and lower pest activity and populations. As an immediate insecticide, the oils coat soft-bodied pests including thrips, spider mites and mealybugs to name a few, blocking breathing holes and smothering them. As a hormone disruptor, neem oil can slow the developmental stages of pests and throw off reproductive cues. As an antifeedant, oils are systemically delivered at soil level and absorbed by the roots into plant parts, making them less palatable for grazing pests.

If using, amend the Homemade Insecticidal Soap Spray (page 66) recipe with one teaspoon of neem oil, first mixing the oil with dish soap before adding this in the spray bottle and filling it with warm water and alcohol. This will help to emulsify the oil and make it spread more readily. Shake well before use and shake the bottle often during use to keep the solution well mixed. Use the mixture immediately, discarding any unused solution. Repeat application as needed until signs of pests are reduced. To avoid burning foliage, use neem oil sparingly on delicate, tender leaf tropicals, such as peace lilies (page 133), ferns (page 105), nerve plants (page 125), mini monstera (page 117), cacti (page 93) and succulents. Patch test a few leaves and observe for any adverse reactions to the solution before spraying the entire plant. Use only 100 percent pure neem oil, free of other ingredients like dyes, perfumes or additives.

Repeat application as needed until signs of pests are reduced. A reduction in pests should be seen after the second or third treatment. As many as three applications, spaced about five to ten days apart, are recommended to target all stages of development. If a reduction in pests is not seen after a month, try an alternative method of pest control by introducing beneficial insects.

STEPS UPON DISCOVERING A HOUSEPLANT PEST

1. Isolate the infected plant from surrounding plants immediately upon discovery of an infestation. Another room with similar conditions to what it previously thrived in would be ideal to avoid airborne or crawling pests from infringing on other plants.

2. Thoroughly rinse debris and pests in a sink, shower or bathtub using a shower attachment or outdoors using the garden hose away from exterior plantings.

3. In a 4-cup (1-L) spray bottle, mix all of the ingredients for the Homemade Insecticidal Soap Spray.

4. Spray liberally, covering all leaf surfaces and crevices as well as soil surfaces. Let sit for fifteen minutes and then rinse off with tepid water.

5. Repeat application (approximately every 7-10 days) as needed until signs of pests are reduced. I like to schedule these treatments on watering days to avoid overwatering my plants.

HOMEMADE INSECTICIDAL SOAP SPRAY

1 tbsp (15 ml) mild dish or castile soap

1 cup (240 ml) Isopropyl alcohol (no higher than 70%)

3 cups (720 ml) water

Beneficial Insects

A convenient and mess-free form of pest prevention, beneficial insects are minute soldiers that hunt down specific pests. Some even prey on multiple developmental stages of pests, thriving and multiplying as long as there is a food source.

Some common beneficial insects used to target pests include: *Neoseiulus californicus* to control spider mites, *Steinernema feltiae* to seek the larvae of fungus gnats, *Cryptolaemus montrouzieri* that will happily feast on mealybugs and *Amblyseius swirskii* to hunt down the larvae and early stages of thrips. Thoroughly read the instructions for use, since proper timing and application procedures will ensure a higher success rate after release. Repeat application to ensure thorough coverage of infected areas, or you may consider using them on a routine basis for pest prevention. These small but mighty scavengers work well and cover a large number of plants, especially when grouped together where foliage is in contact with another.

Purchase beneficial insects from reputable distributors—either through the web (see koppert.com) or at garden centers—and bear in mind that transit conditions from either mail orders or travel to and from retailers can affect the efficacy of these live organisms. Carefully read the instructions for use prior to purchasing the beneficial insects and release them shortly after they're in your possession. Refrain from using neem treatments or other forms of pesticides several weeks before the introduction of beneficial insects.

Adult predatory mites such as this Amblyseius swirskii prey on immature stages of various thrips species.

DISEASES

Root Rot

An overwatered plant with consistently waterlogged soil makes the perfect breeding ground for harmful fungal pathogens to fester. The tell-tale signs of this number one plant killer begin covertly underground, attacking the root system: blackened roots rendered into mush, wilting from the bottom up, foul-smelling roots or plant parts and yellow, brown or blackened leaves. By the time root rot has set in and the root system is diminished, it is more than likely unsalvageable.

However, if there is a presence of some healthy—typically firm and white—roots remaining, you can try to save the plant by first carefully removing all of the decomposed parts using sharp scissors and then discarding the contaminated soil. Soaking the affected plant in a basin of water can help dislodge remnants of the soil and decayed debris. Place the wet plant on top of some paper towels and let it air-dry slightly. Repot it in fresh substrate using a mix that is appropriate for the species. Place the weakened plant in a warm and brightly lit area that is free from direct sun and withhold watering for twice as long as you would normally wait to water. Adding a small amount of hydrogen peroxide when watering can help further eliminate and prevent the spread of pathogens. Resume a regular watering schedule once you see signs of improvement.

Prevent root rot by using an appropriate mix of substrates for the specimen (see page 39), providing adequate drainage. The presence of drainage holes on the bottom of a planter can immensely decrease the likelihood of overwatering. Water only when your plant baby is thirsty and use a moisture meter if you are unsure—read more on that on page 35. Or, depending on the type of plant, most can tolerate—and some even prefer—to dry out slightly between waterings. Be sure there is enough light provided for the plant to undergo photosynthesis. Amending a small handful of activated charcoal into the soil mix can also provide some prevention of fungal growth.

Healthy roots   *Roots affected by root rot*

Other Diseases

Less common diseases include powdery mildew, gray mold and black spots. Signs to look for that indicate the possibility of disease include but are not limited to: white residue, fuzzy growth and black or brown spots on leaves with a yellow halo. Isolate the plant to prevent the spread of contagious diseases to other surrounding plants. Prune no more than one-third of the most affected areas. Spray the specimen with a prepared Homemade Insecticidal Soap Spray (page 66) to kill and prevent further spread of pathogens. Prevent future outbreaks by increasing air circulation and avoid pooling of water on leaf surfaces. Provide appropriate temperatures and humidity, as well as proper watering amounts and frequencies to further help combat the spread of these diseases.

Parting Notes on Pests + Diseases

Always inspect plants for the presence of pests and diseases before introducing them into the home environment. Since this is sometimes difficult to detect before buying, it would be wise to quarantine any new acquisitions for several weeks to observe for signs of bugs, preventing the possibility of contaminating other household plants. The best defense to prevent unwanted pests and diseases is to recognize signs of unwanted pests and their activity, remove decayed plant material regularly and regulate your environment and the resources you give your plants.

Remember a sick plant needs time to recoup and any repotting, heavy pruning, fertilizing or extreme changes in environments should be avoided until full recovery. Unfortunately, sometimes you just have to cut your losses and discard heavily infested or sick plants. Go ahead and repurchase the same plant or try something new—the fun and enjoyment stems from the survivors who stay and thrive in your care.

PLANT PARENTING TIP

Memorize the three R's to prevent pests and diseases:

- **Recognize** signs of pest activity, isolate and treat infestations as soon as they are discovered.

- **Remove** dead and decaying plant matter on a regular basis. Avoid propagating or bringing home infected plants. This also means throwing out severely infected plants!

- **Regulate** your environment and resources. You control the delicate balance between light, water and humidity, temperature, substrate and nutrients to help your plants thrive.

POTTING

One of the most frequently asked questions is: "When should I repot my plant?" There are many factors that come into play when it comes to "repotting" or "potting up" a plant. "Repotting" is a widely used phrase that encompasses the process of providing your plant with fresh soil or an amendment of the substrate, whether you are reusing the existing container or one of a different material and, of course, size. "Potting up" your plant, as the phrase suggests, involves upgrading your plant to a larger container size.

Buying from a reputable distributor means you can bring home and leave the plant as-is, in its current container and substrate. You can trust that your new acquisition has been provided with an adequately sized container, typically in a plastic nursery pot, in a soil mixture or substrate suitable for the particular species. Additionally, there may even already be an amendment of fertilizer in the substrate, as you can sometimes notice by the small rounded pellets scattered in the soil.

Another benefit to leaving the plant untouched, as mentioned in the Acquisition chapter (page 9), is that a new plant can experience shock from a change of environment—from the greenhouse to your home, for example—and a procedure such as repotting would add additional strain on the acclimating specimen.

If you want to place your newly acquired plant baby in a decorative, also known as "cache," pot, then simply place the plant in its nursery pot right into it. This double-potting method works well for swapping out decorative planters and as a way to keep runoff from damaging surfaces while watering. Some planters have drainage holes with catch-trays or saucers for this reason—just remember to discard stagnant water to prevent a favorable environment for fungus gnats to thrive.

When to Repot or Pot-Up

Resist repotting a newly acquired plant until it is necessary to perform such a taxing task on the specimen. Repot or pot-up if one or more of the following scenarios apply to the specimen in question:

Visual Symptoms

When a plant should be repotted is largely based on whether the roots have become "root-bound," that is, when the root system has outgrown its container and has therefore exhausted both its nutrients and substrate. The first signs of a root-bound plant that can benefit from an upgrade can be seen externally—roots may be seen pushing through drainage holes or even above the soil's surface, bulging on the sides of a plastic container and the plant may exhibit rapidly wilting and yellowing leaves from the bottom-up.

Weight Distribution

A top-heavy plant that keeps tipping over would be another situation to cause a repot. Upgrade the container size slightly, opting for planters with added weight—think concrete, cement, stone, plaster and terracotta. These can all help add stability. Amending the soil with substrates such as pumice, sand or bark can also help bulk up the medium. Alternatively, lining the bottom of the planter with stones can help add additional weight and drainage.

Incorrect Medium

If you bring home a new plant and the pot feels heavy from watering, see that this moisture is used up by the specimen in a timely matter. Unfortunately, not all suppliers are equal in the quality of substrates the plants are sold in and sometimes plants are found growing in waterlogged dirt. If the roots stay soggy for too long, fungal growth sets in, rendering the precious foundation of your plant to a pulp. Definitely repot your plant baby in an appropriate medium in this situation.

Soil Compaction

Yet another reason to repot comes from the fact that over time, organic matter such as peat moss will decompose and compact. This causes suffocation of the roots, shrinking them and leading to the demise of the plant. Always add an amendment of slowly decomposing substrate like perlite or pumice, coco chips or bark to the organic matter to help provide air pockets allowing the roots to breathe.

Infestation

If you have confirmed that there is an infestation of pests or disease that have infiltrated the soil, then perform a repot. Signs of an infestation include the presence of eggs, larvae or pests. Carefully remove and discard all contaminated soil from the root ball. Determine an appropriate course of action after reviewing the Diagnostics section (see page 57) to identify, control and prevent further spread of pests or disease.

How to Repot

Once you have acquired a new planter, nursery liner and potting mix (see page 51) appropriate for the upgrade, carefully remove the plant from the liner. Firmly hold the base of the specimen close to the soil line with one hand and squeeze the sides of the liner to free the root ball with the other. If you are having a difficult time freeing the root ball from its container, cut the liner, being careful not to cut the roots when doing so.

With the root ball now exposed, take this opportunity to get a little messy and dabble with the contents of the soil and root mass. Observe for signs of pest activity, the presence of mold growth and more importantly the general health and anatomy of the root structure. As a general rule of thumb, healthy roots should be off-white to tan in color, firm and abundant. If the roots are crumbly, brown to black in color or easily fall off when you pull at them, you may be dealing with root rot. See page 68 on how to manage this.

For robust plants like a monstera (page 121) with hardy roots, you can tease away the old soil with your fingers, a small hand rake or cultivator to help with the process. Smaller or sensitive plants with delicate roots like nerve plants (page 125) or radiator plants (page 145) should have extra care taken when removing soil from the root ball. Loosen as much of the soil as possible without damaging the roots and leave some old soil intact if you have to.

As a general rule of thumb, discard all previously used soil, especially in the case of an infestation or soil degradation, which is when the soil's nutrients have been expended and the ratio of soil to roots cannot sustain the plant. Occasionally, I will reuse existing soil during a repotting of a newly purchased plant and top up with fresh substrate because it will still be nutrient-dense. This process may also lessen the chance of shock from the procedure and new soil composition.

If you are strictly refreshing the soil or if you wish to keep your plant growth minimal and are reusing the same planter or nursery liner, determine if the root ball requires a trim. If the root system has encircled the bottom and taken the shape of the container, it can benefit from a small trim. Gently detangle the mass and trim it using sharp, clean scissors, snipping any lengthy pieces.

If the drainage holes in your planter or nursery liner are large and you want to avoid substrate from draining through during watering, you can place a sheet of garden fabric or coffee filters (pictured below) cut to size in the base of the pot. Measure the amount of soil needed to cover the bottom of the pot by placing the plant into the center of the planter with the crown—where stem meets roots—aligned several inches below the rim of the planter. Backfill the pot with fresh mix, pressing the medium firmly as you fill. Keep filling until the substrate covers the entire root ball up to the original soil line.

Water thoroughly to allow the medium to settle and fill with more mix if needed. Plants such as cacti (page 93) and succulents and those that were recently watered don't need to be watered right away and may even prefer to be left alone until acclimated to the new substrate. If you choose, top-dress with bark, mulch, decorative stone, sand or sphagnum moss.

Once you have repotted your plant, expect some level of transplant shock, as your green baby recuperates from the procedure and acclimates to the new medium. Refrain from exposing your newly potted plant to extreme environmental fluctuations, fertilizing or intense pruning until it is fully recovered and acclimated. Practice repotting on a case-by-case basis, observing if and when your plant baby needs a new container and fresh medium.

Tips for Repotting Success

Container Size

If the repot coincides with an upgrade in pot size, only size up by an inch or two (2.5 or 5 cm). "Over-potting" occurs when a sudden influx of substrate disrupts watering habits and photosynthesis. This occurs because more soil means greater water retention, which the plant cannot efficiently use up, creating a waterlogged environment. This leads to issues like fungus gnats and, in severe cases, root rot. Being modest when upgrading your pot size can help ease them into their new home.

Lifestyle

If you know you're a trigger-happy waterer and tend to shower your green babies with too much love, then you may opt for a terracotta pot to help water absorption. If your schedule does not allow you to water your plants on a weekly basis, potting up slightly, thereby increasing soil content, can better suit an occasional plant parent who prefers infrequent watering duties. You may opt to find the perfect soil mixture coupled with the perfect container size to better align all the plants to a matching watering schedule.

Timing

The best time to perform repotting projects is ideally in the spring and summer when plants are at their healthiest, most robust growing stage. This timeframe will allow a stressed-out plant experiencing shock from repotting to recoup and adjust itself more readily to the new planter and fresh substrate. Anytime outside of this suggested timeframe is fine, provided that you pay closer attention to your watering habits, as your plant may be in its resting stage and preferring not to be disturbed. Doing so may weaken the plant causing it to be more prone to pest or fungal infestations.

PLANT PARENTING TIP

Premeasure the diameter of your nursery pot before décor shopping, ensuring the depth of the decorative planter will be tall enough to house the plant in its nursery liner. Propping up the plant within the cache pot will not only give you more control of how the plant sits and ultimately looks as a whole, but will also prevent overwatering by protecting the boosted plant from any residual water that comes through the drainage hole—just be sure to discard this extra water. Use foraged items like stones or reuse single-use plastics like food containers to prop up a plant.

Unpropped plant. Look for foraged items in the home, like these takeout containers to elevate the look of a plant.

A propped up plant not only elevates the look of it, but can also prevent overwatering by allowing the excess water to drain more readily into the cache pot.

PROPAGATION

There is great fulfillment in creating or owning something that you can observe thriving under the care and attention you provide it. If you are or have ever been a parent of a dog, cat, fish or human baby, then you know the gratification in the ability to influence their health, well-being and happiness—plant ownership or plant parenthood can be seen in a similar vein.

Some time has passed and you've grown quite fond of your plant baby—a parental instinct calls from within and you want more of these green babies! Sure, you can go out and simply buy another plant, but where's the fun and challenge in that? If you've got a thriving and healthy plant due to the time and attention you gave it, then try your hand at cloning and multiplying it. They make great gifts for friends and family and think of the extra cash you would save—to buy more plants in the future, of course.

Plant propagation is the method by which new plants are created from a parent specimen. There are four propagation types for producing new plants—sexual, asexual, layering and grafting. The most convenient and preferred mechanism for multiplying houseplants is through asexual vegetative reproduction using individual or a combination of plant parts such as leaves, stems and roots. Some of the easy and commonly used propagation techniques include divisions and cuttings. In this next section, we'll go over what each one entails and how to pull them off successfully.

Tools + Materials for Propagating Projects

Sharp knife or gardening shears

Small nursery pots

Small glass jars

Small trowel

Tweezers

Ziplock bags, plastic domes or takeout containers

Rooting hormone (optional)

Division

Division is a method of creating new plants by breaking off whole sections of a parent plant with roots and crown intact. Begin by removing the plant from the pot and use your fingers to massage the substrate to gently separate and loosen roots. Using a clean, sharp knife or pruning shears, cut any horizontal stems and intertwined roots to help with the separation process. Repot new sections in fresh substrate. Use this method on large, upright and mature specimens for species such as peace lilies (page 133), snake plants (page 153) and ferns (page 105).

Division is a method also used on newly emerged baby plants—also known as pups, offsets or plantlets—attached to the mother plant. Without the need to remove the entire plant out of its pot, firmly and carefully pluck the pups from the parent plant. If this is not feasible, use a sharp knife or small trowel to help. This method works great for plants such as haworthias (page 113), echeverias (page 101) and snake plants (page 153). On mature spider plants (page 157), small plantlets form on the flowering ends of runners that can then be cut and easily rooted either in water or soil.

Cuttings

By far the most popular technique with a high success rate, propagation by cuttings can be achieved using a variety of plant parts taken from the parent plant such as nodes, stems and leaves. Nodes and stem cuttings can be placed either in water or soil to root, while leaves are usually rooted into a potting medium.

Cut ½ inch (1.3 cm) or more below a node, where the leaf and stem meet, from the tip of a vine, leaving one to three leaves intact for photosynthesis. Fill your container of choice with filtered rain or tap water that has been left overnight or a sterile, soilless potting medium if rooting in soil. Using sharp clean shears, ensure that any foliage sitting below the substrate is removed to prevent rot. Leaving a cutting out to air-dry slightly until the ends callous over can prevent stem rot and slightly boost the efficacy of rooting. At least one node must be in the substrate as this is where roots will emerge. Vining plants such as various pothos (page 141), philodendrons (page 137), string of hearts (page 161) and monsteras (page 121) work well with this technique.

Leaf cuttings, usually a blade with a small portion of the petiole (the stalk that connects the leaf to the stem) and in some cases, segments of the blade, can be placed in a sterile starting medium for this technique. Sphagnum peat moss, vermiculate or a soilless mix all work. Place a small, even bed of your medium in a shallow pot, or even a repurposed takeout container, and place the blade on top. Like that of regular stem cuttings, let the leaf with the cut end callous slightly before inserting into the potting medium. Keep the medium moist to start and establish a watering schedule once a sizable plant emerges. Try this technique with plants such as radiator plants with the petiole (page 145) and echeveria leaves (page 101).

Some plants can be propagated via segments of stems, free of leaves. With a clean, sharp knife, cut several inches of stem to ensure that at least one node is included. Insert the cut parts into water or a sterile starting medium. This propagation technique is best reserved for thick-stemmed cane type plants such as corn plants (page 97).

Rooting in water typically yields faster results compared to soil and using a clear container allows you to monitor rooting activity. A slight disadvantage to water-rooting is that the plant can suffer from transplant stress upon transferring it to a potting medium. Timing or root-stage is also crucial to successfully acclimate a water-rooted cutting into soil. Generally speaking, you want to see at least ½ inch (1.3 cm) of roots for small plants and up to several inches in larger ones before transplanting.

When the rooted specimen is ready to be potted, opt for a small nursery pot to start, allowing you to closely monitor moisture levels and for the roots to find their footing quicker. Use a suitable mix for the species and keep the soil moist, but not wet, for the next month or so until the roots have acclimated to the new substrate. Give the baby plant a light tug every several weeks to gauge resistance and watch for new growth—favorable signs that the specimen is rooting and adapting. Establish a regular watering schedule thereafter.

CAN PLANTS SURVIVE INDEFINITELY IN WATER?

Yes! Some plants like spider plants (page 157), pothos (page 141) and philodendrons (page 137) can survive exclusively in water, never having to deal with soil and some of the blunders it may come with. This gives you the flexibility to use any waterproof vessel you choose, so get creative! Be sure to change the water when it becomes cloudy and use opaque containers to prevent algae growth. Most importantly, because the water lacks nutrients plants need, feed the plant with small amounts of water-soluble fertilizer or soil conditioners.

Bear in mind that every species has differing rooting timeframes, with some like pothos (page 141) putting out roots within a week and others like a ficus tree (page 109) taking at least a month's time before showing any activity. Some species, especially those with variegation—that is, plant parts varying in appearance or color—may be more difficult to propagate and can even revert back to their green variants.

A gentle reminder that not all propagation trials result in success, but when you eventually do discover roots or new growth from your efforts, it will be quite rewarding! Keep trying and experiment with different methods with a variety of plants you own.

Tips for Propagation Success

Always use healthy, mature plant parts, free of pests and diseases to increase success rate.

The use of a rooting hormone is optional and can sometimes help speed up and encourage, but not guarantee, rooting ability. They can be purchased in powder, gel or liquid form in both natural and synthetic formats.

Keeping tools sanitized, working on a clean surface and avoiding double-dipping in rooting hormone are ways to prevent the possible spread of bacteria and disease to your vulnerable cuttings.

When propagating in soil, be sure to insert the plant parts in the same orientation they were grown—any other position will stunt, deform or cease growth. Propagation can be done any time of the year, but spring is preferred, when most plants are growing at their optimal and robust stage—this period of time will help speed regenerative growth and development as well.

Rooting success will vary between individual cuttings, so increase your chances by propagating in abundance to create a fuller looking plant.

Place newly propagated babies in a warm, bright and indirectly lit area.

Increase rooting success by elevating humidity levels—place the propagated plant in a ziplock bag or cover with a plastic dome, removing these coverings every so often to increase air circulation.

Refresh the water in water-propagated plants when it becomes cloudy. Soil-propagated plants should be kept evenly moist until they are established and new growth appears.

Commence a regular watering and feeding schedule once the plant is showing establishment with new growth.

It is important to establish newly propagated plants before passing them on to friends and family to ensure the best start to acclimating in their new homes.

HERO HOUSEPLANTS

There are a plethora of shapes and sizes when it comes to houseplants, and it may be intimidating at first to decide what will suit your needs. Before you commit to a plant that you've decided looks great, you want to first and foremost assess the availability of light in a given space. Use your best judgment armed with The Principles of Care covered on pages 21 to 85 and start experimenting with a few small, inexpensive plants.

When some time has passed and your new green babies appear to have acclimated themselves to their new home or you notice some new growth appearing, you will gain a sense of confidence in your plant parenting skills and may even feel empowered to make additions to the plant family. It is absolutely normal and natural to feel the urge to want to buy every plant you come across, but I suggest taking things slow and steady in order to truly enjoy your new journey to becoming a plant parent.

This chapter is a list of great looking houseplants that, in some instances, will forgive you if you miss a watering or two and many won't fuss for not having a window seat, some even thriving on neglect. These plants won't break the bank or demand constant attention. In time, with patience and observation, you will learn to get a sense of what makes them stay alive and ultimately, thrive in your growing collection. These are the Hero Houseplants.

Size + Growth Habit: 5 feet (1.5 m) tall + upright
Toxicity Level: mildly toxic when ingested

BIRDS OF PARADISE
Strelitzia

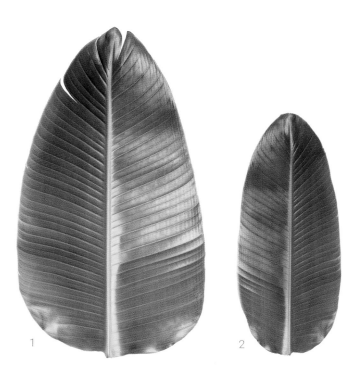

1
2

If you want to immerse yourself with tropical vacation vibes year round, look no further than the coveted bird of paradise, named after the bird-like ornate orange and blue flowers produced by this South African native tropical. Don't be alarmed if your bird of paradise does not develop the blooms they are known for. It is not uncommon for them to not bloom at all when grown indoors. Despite this drawback, a bird of paradise will reward you with impressively large oblong leaves erect from sturdy petioles. This heat-loving big bird will thrive best in lots of light, happily basking in southern exposed sun.

1. Nicolai
2. Reginae

HOW TO STYLE

Elevate your tropical retreat with a bird of paradise situated in a brightly lit room—think beside south- or west-facing windows—and let the stately leaf blades canopy over a sitting or lounging area. Create a big impact by pairing the big bird with a tall planter further emphasizing its height; alternatively, prop the bird of paradise in a shorter planter atop a sturdy stand to create extra height. When it comes to planters, look for patterns, colors and textures that mimic natural materials: wood, concrete, stone, marble and clay in neutral colors are great options to create warmth while promoting a sense of the great outdoors. The large broad leaves of these bird of paradise plants require dusting as a regular form of maintenance, not only to keep them looking their best, but to also allow optimal photosynthesis.

BASIC CARE

Light
Bright indirect to direct sun.

Water
Water thoroughly when soil is almost dry to dry. Tolerates occasional drought. Enjoys humidity.

Substrate
Well-draining, tropical mix (page 51).

Nutrients
Slow-release, water-soluble as new growth appears. Feel free to feed this robust and hungry plant throughout the year.

Common Problem
This plant is very susceptible to spider mites. If you spot signs of spider mites (see page 64), quarantine the plant, moving it away from all other houseplants. Bring it into the shower or tub and treat with a Homemade Insecticidal Soap Spray (page 66).

FUN FACT
The bird of paradise gets its name from the extravagant blossoms they produce, varying in colors from orange, white and yellow and resembling the silhouette of an exotic bird.

While the thought of cacti summons visions of sandy arid deserts, these slow-growing spiny succulents can thrive in the household environment too. If you have bright direct sunlight coming from south- or west-facing windows, cacti will live happily close to these sources of light. There is a myriad of sizes, colors and shapes—flat, spherical, columnar, even some tree-like—to suit every plant parent's individual style.

1. Fairy Castle
2. Blue Columnar
3. Golden Barrel
4. Peruvian Old Lady
5. Parodia Yellow Tower
6. Pincushion
7. Bunny Ear

HOW TO STYLE

Cacti look great on their own in individual pots. Terracotta or clay pots complement these desert dwellers well in addition to being a little more forgiving to a heavy watering hand. However, have some fun composing mini desert vignettes by grouping contrasting shapes, sizes and textures in a shallow planter with the addition of natural elements like stones and driftwood. In a similar vein, you can compose an arrangement with cacti's high light-loving cousin succulents, which share similar care, housing them in a contained environment by building a terrarium. Top-dressing with sand or pebbles not only elevates the desert vibe, but also helps wick moisture away from the base of the plant.

BASIC CARE

Light
Bright indirect to direct light.

Water
Water thoroughly when soil is completely dry. Tolerates drought well.

Substrate
Cactus mix (page 51).

Nutrients
Does not need fertilizer to thrive.

Common Problem
Rot occurs from overwatering. It is a bacterial or fungal infection marked by soft, mushy plant parts and roots. If the roots have rotted away, but the remaining specimen is unaffected, remove as much of the damaged roots as possible, allowing the plant to dry off as much as possible; replant in fresh cactus mix (page 51) and cut back on the watering frequency.

FUN FACT
All cacti are succulents, but not all succulents are cacti. Areoles are areas of the cactus where spikes and flowers arise and are the defining feature of cacti.

Size + Growth Habit: 2–12 inches (5–30 cm) tall + compact rosette
Toxicity Level: nontoxic

ECHEVERIAS
Echeveria

A genus of well over 150 species, echeverias are mostly found in dry to semi-arid rocky areas of Central America, Mexico and northwestern South America. One of the most adored and elegant succulents, they are loved for their compact rosette form and if given ideal conditions, will reward you with spikes of flowers many times over the course of their life. Being easy and fun to propagate either by leaf cuttings (page 82) or offsets (page 81) makes caring for this plant a very rewarding experience. This is a great low-maintenance beginner's plant for the forgetful plant parent who may miss watering days, thriving well on neglect and lack of extra care and attention.

1. Lola
2. Parva
3. Topsy Turvy
4. Apus
5. Perle Von Nurnberg
6. Purpusorum
7. Imbricata Blue Rose

HOW TO STYLE

Provided that you supply echeverias with adequate amounts—think lots—of bright light, they will thrive beautifully in their compact formations and vibrant colors in whatever container you arrange them in. Select a variety of rosettes and place them in a row of repeating matching planters on the windowsill of a north-, south- or east-facing window—and a west-facing window in the winter—and watch them blush in vibrant colors as they bask in the sun. Arrange a contrasting assortment of echeverias with other succulents and cacti of similar care in a terrarium, the portability of which will allow you to move this little ecosystem around the home for various light exposures and styling purposes. Repurpose a deep dish or decorative bowl and make a summer succulent platter for a unique coffee or dining table centerpiece.

BASIC CARE

Light
Bright light to full sun.

Water
Water thoroughly only when soil is dry. Tolerates drought.

Substrate
Cactus mix (page 51). Do not overpot.

Nutrients
Does not require any extra nutrients to thrive well. Use a very diluted organic soil enhancer or minimal amounts of worm casting if desired.

Common Problem
Since echeveria requires bright light, etiolation can occur if the plant is starved of light and begins to seek brighter light sources. This is marked by elongated and sometimes weakened stems, sparse small or dropping lower leaves and loss of color. Salvage and propagate healthy parts of the plant (see page 79) and move the newly potted plants to a brighter location.

FUN FACT
The genus *Echeveria* was named in honor of Atanasio Echeverría y Godoy, an eighteenth-century Mexican botanical artist and naturalist who trained at the Royal Art Academy in Mexico.

Size + Growth Habit: upwards of 3 feet (1 m) tall + epiphytic, rhizomatous
Toxicity Level: nontoxic

These classic humid-loving ornamentals, characterized by their compound arrangement of long and lacy fronds, instantly add a touch of the outdoors. With a wide variety of styling options, whether hanging, in a terrarium or bathroom, there's a fern that will thrive in many situations once you learn a balance of its needs to keep it happy.

1. Rabbit's Foot
2. Maidenhair
3. Boston
4. Fluffly Ruffle
5. Crocodile
6. Victoria Bird's Nest
7. Lemon Button

HOW TO STYLE

Smaller specimens like the button and asparagus ferns are suitable options for closed terrariums, which provide that consistently humid environment they love so much. Combine several species of ferns with other terrarium appropriate plants like the nerve plant (page 125) and radiator plants (page 145) for textural contrast and variety. Grouping several ferns together will increase humidity as well, and placing this grouping in a bathroom will further boost the balmy ambiance they natively thrive in. In other less humid situations, use a room humidifier or place a potted fern on top of a pebble tray filled with water to allow the evaporation to generate some humidity. At the very least, mist regularly to keep the delicate leaves looking fresh and green.

BASIC CARE

Light
Medium to bright indirect or dappled light. Low light tolerable. Do not expose to direct sun for long periods of time.

Water
Water thoroughly when soil is almost dry, keeping the medium moist at all times. Enjoys consistent humidity; mist daily.

Substrate
Well-draining, tropical mix (page 51) with added sand.

Nutrients
Diluted, water-soluble as new growth appears.

Common Problem
Browning, loss of color, or crispy leaves are commonly experienced with ferns, especially in average temperate household environments where humidity may be low. Maintain moist soil by watering thoroughly as soon as the soil has dried out and not letting the plant sit bone-dry for long periods. Misting frequently, using a room humidifier, placing the fern in the bathroom, using a pebble tray, double-potting with moist sphagnum in a cache pot with the potted fern fit into it are all methods to help increase humidity.

FUN FACT
A widely cultivated houseplant, the fern group of over 10,000 known species is regarded as one of the oldest plants, with fossil records dating back to more than 360 million years ago.

Size + Growth Habit: 6–10 feet (2–3 m) tall + upright and tree-like
Toxicity Level: toxic when ingested, sap causes skin irritation

FICUS TREES
Ficus

The understated granddad of indoor trees, some ficus trees will display without complaint, in low light—not to be mistaken for no light—areas of the home. Available in a great variety of sizes, you will enjoy any stage of this faithful plant. Start small as a desktop piece to give those working eyes a break and watch it grow into a statement stand-alone veteran, towering in a common room. Expect some repotting projects for this one, so get ready to get your hands dirty (see page 71).

1. Burgundy
2. Tineke
3. Lyrata
4. Audrey
5. Altissima
6. Audrey Golden

HOW TO STYLE

The ficus tree lends itself to a modern yet timeless display, pairing well with a simple matte white planter to create a bold contrast against the deep green elliptical leaves of the burgundy cultivar. Try a smaller specimen placed on a tabletop and observe its needs and preferences; they tend to respond with a respectable amount of feedback. A medium-sized plant can offer multiple vantage points around the house as it increases in size and its needs for space evolve. Enjoy the versatility of this plant on its quest around the home, creating multiple looks—from a small tabletop specimen that transforms into a towering floor piece. For larger specimens, opt for a sizable planter to anchor the stately plant. Staking it with supports such as natural gardening bamboo sticks will stabilize the weight of an aging plant and give it a more tree-like appearance.

BASIC CARE

Light
Medium to bright indirect or dappled light. Low light tolerable. Should not be exposed to any direct sunlight.

Water
Water thoroughly when soil is almost dry to dry. Tolerates occasional drought. Enjoys humidity.

Substrate
Well-draining, chunky mix with lots of orchid bark. Mix in sand to stabilize the plant and prevent it from falling over as it grows.

Nutrients
Slow-release, water-soluble as new growth appears.

Common Problem
A drooping ficus tree marked by curling leaves could mean it is not being watered sufficiently. If it is being watered regularly and is marked by yellowing and dropping leaves, let the plant dry out and increase the number of days in your watering schedule. Drastic changes in care—for example, prolonged periods of drought—can result in deformities in the development of new leaves.

FUN FACT
The ficus tree is commonly known as the rubber plant because it produces a milky white latex that was once used to make rubber products.

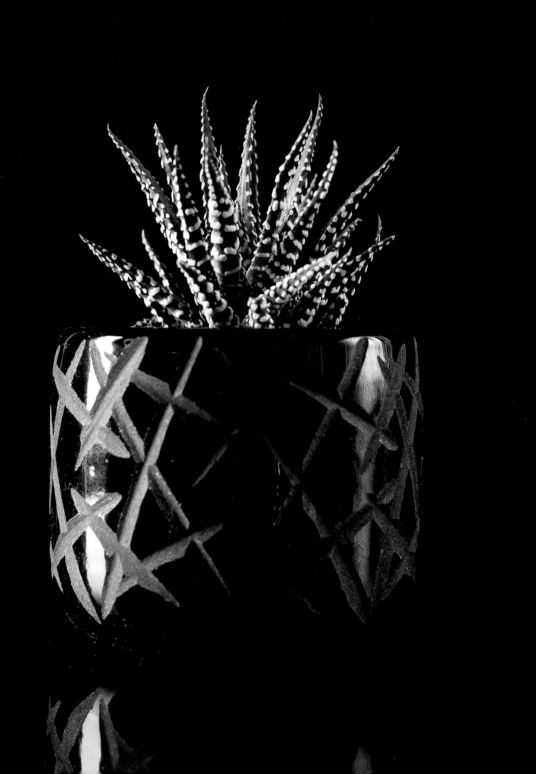

Size + Growth Habit: upwards of 5 inches (13 cm) tall + clumping
Toxicity Level: nontoxic

HAWORTHIAS
Haworthia

1   2   3   4   5

A slow-growing rosette-forming semitropical, often distinguished by striking white tubercles on tightly packed pointed leaves, the haworthia is the quintessential beginner plant parent's succulent. Thriving in a range of full sun to lower light situations and neglect, this small stemless plant does not bring about many issues, provided that you do not overwater it. Provide it with more light to promote the white markings and patterns—some will also blush with reddish hues. Divide offsets, or "pups," to make more plants or share them with friends and family—see page 81.

1. Retusa
2. Wandera Miami
3. Fasciata
4. Attenuata
5. Venosa Tessallata

HOW TO STYLE

Haworthias' slow-growth, compact size and easy-going nature make them ideal for open-top terrariums or dainty containers. Search around the home for small teacups, shot glasses or empty candle jars and either drop the plant, still in the nursery pot, right into these cache pots or make sure to include a drainage layer for vessels without drainage holes if you are repotting—see page 76. Highlight the white textural tubercles by pairing these drought tolerant plants with simple white planters topped with white gravel, peppering these pots wherever the home needs a pop of warmth. Compose a semidesert platter using a shallow dish with multiple specimens clumped together top-dressed with sand, rock and sun-bleached driftwood for a unique coffee table arrangement or centerpiece.

BASIC CARE

Light
Medium to bright indirect or dappled light, tolerating a few hours of direct sun each day. Low light tolerable.

Water
Water thoroughly when soil is dry. Tolerates occasional drought.

Substrate
Cactus mix (page 51).

Nutrients
Does not require extra nutrients to thrive. However, a diluted water-soluble fertilizer can be used with the presence of active growth.

Common Problem
Root rot is the number one killer for succulents. To avoid this, water only when the soil has completely dried, using your senses as described on page 31 to help determine when this is. A rotting haworthia may show signs of dropping leaves, a mushy base or the plant lifting easily from the substrate. If the plant is not too far gone and some of the leaves and core have not completely withered away, remove as much of the affected parts as possible and repot the core in fresh cactus soil. Refrain from watering for the next few weeks to allow it to recover before resuming a watering schedule.

FUN FACT
The tubercles allow expansion of the leaf during the moister summer months, without imparting any tearing or damage to the stiff epidermal surfaces.

Size + Growth Habit: upwards of 12 feet (4 m) tall + vining
Toxicity Level: mildly toxic when ingested

MINI MONSTERA
Rhaphidophora tetrasperma

Despite the mini monstera's many aliases, it is neither a monstera (page 121) nor a philodendron (page 137), although it does share characteristics from both genera. For example, the mini monstera undergoes metamorphosis during its structural leaf development comparable to philodendrons. Metamorphosis is defined as the change in leaf shape or other plant parts during their development as a result of their environment. As these same leaves mature, they will fenestrate just like the fan favorite, fast-growing monstera. With easy care requirements just like its monstera and philodendron doppelgängers, the mini monstera is a great beginner's plant for those entering plant parenthood. Be prepared to supply this nimble grower with some kind of support like a bamboo stick as it takes off in vertical space.

Above are four independent leaf formations from the same specimen as a result of metamorphosis—the change in leaf-shape or other plant parts during its development affected by the environment.

HOW TO STYLE

Fancy the deeply lobed leaves of the notorious monstera but don't have the real estate for this hefty plant? Opt for the svelte profile of the mini monstera, great for small spaces and compact living quarters. Get creative with support while adding texture and movement around the home—train the growing vine around a large round mirror, create a conversation piece with a unique mini monstera halo or grow it up as an otherwise bare column using invisible cable clips to support the vines. This hardy houseplant has a will to live, so don't be afraid to prune back overgrown vines, making sure to keep the cuttings for more plants—see more on page 82! Simplicity is key to styling this plant, especially in its mature form with its quirky lobed leaves, so let it take center stage when styling a vignette.

BASIC CARE

Light
Medium to bright indirect or dappled light, tolerating a few hours of direct sun each day. Low light tolerable.

Water
Water thoroughly when soil is almost dry to dry. Tolerates occasional drought. Enjoys humidity.

Substrate
Well-draining, chunky or tropical mix (page 51).

Nutrients
Slow-release, water-soluble as new growth appears. Feel free to feed this robust and hungry plant throughout the year.

Common Problem
Lack of splits in leaves. A juvenile mini monstera, much like its larger *Monstera deliciosa* cousin, will start off with ovate-shaped leaves and the absence of fenestrations. Give it lots of bright, indirect light and within a few years and some leaf turnover, expect those prized splits and sometimes even miniature holes. If you already have a large mature plant and the leaves are not producing fenestrations, gradually move the plant to a brighter spot.

FUN FACT
Although the mini monstera looks like a smaller version of the monstera, which is native to Central America, it is actually endemic to Southern Thailand and Malaysia.

Size + Growth Habit: upwards of 33 feet (10 m) tall + sprawling
Toxicity Level: mildly toxic when ingested

MONSTERAS
Monstera

A fast-climbing tropical, some monsteras can quickly take over a space creating that jungle vibe. If space permits, let it spread as it grows for a wild untamed look. For smaller spaces and a polished look, train the vines to grow up a support pole. If given enough light, some monsteras will reward you with deeply lobed leaves and fenestrations, those predetermined lobes and holes on the leaves which serve to withstand high winds and rain in the wild. Forgiving in nature and adaptable, look for one of the many monstera varieties that suits your style and décor sense.

1. Deliciosa
2. Thai Constellation
3. Peru
4. Dubia
5. Adansonii

HOW TO STYLE

A *Monstera deliciosa* makes a great stand-alone statement piece on the floor of a large, open room. When grouped together where the monstera is the focal point plant, you can place it together with other large potted plants of contrasting leaf sizes and shapes, like a tall pothos totem (page 141) and a mature snake plant (page 153). For convenience of care and style harmony, group monsteras of different varieties like the *Monstera adansonii* and Thai constellation. Over time, maturing plants will grow long aerial roots. Leave them to grow, trim them or redirect these robust roots back into the pot for added stability—anything goes and none of these methods will cause harm to the plant. For a polished looking plant, or if space is limited, tie the vines to a moss pole to train the monstera to grow vertically.

BASIC CARE

Light
Medium to bright indirect or dappled light, tolerating a few hours of direct sun each day. Low light tolerable. Rotate often to create even growth.

Water
Water thoroughly when soil is almost dry to dry. Tolerates occasional drought. Enjoys humidity.

Substrate
Well-draining, chunky mix.

Nutrients
Slow-release, water-soluble as new growth appears. Feel free to feed this robust and hungry plant throughout the year.

Common Problem
Lack of splits and holes in leaves. A juvenile monstera plant will start off with heart-shaped leaves and the absence of fenestrations. Give it lots of bright, indirect light and within a few years and some leaf turnover, expect those prized splits and holes. If you already have a large mature plant and the leaves are not producing fenestrations, gradually move the plant to a brighter spot.

FUN FACT
In the wild, fenestrations serve to withstand wind and heavy rains as the elements pass through these holes.

Size + Growth Habit: 3–6 inches (8–15 cm) tall + creeping
Toxicity Level: nontoxic

NERVE PLANTS
Fittonia

The nerve plant is nicknamed so for its striking venation against deep green foliage, with veining also found in vibrant colorations like bright pink and red. Though this genus can be considered somewhat temperamental—dramatically drooping when it's thirsty or suffering from leaf crisp—with a little care and attention, the fickle *Fittonia* is resilient in nature and can bounce back with ease. Pinching back lengthy stems can keep this little drama queen in its bushy form, whilst saving the tips to make more babies.

1. Pink Angel
2. Superba
3. Ruby Red

HOW TO STYLE

Due to the nerve plant's compact size and love for humidity, they make perfect candidates for terrariums, paired with other rainforest dwelling plants found on the forest floor like ferns (page 105), mosses and radiator plants (page 145). Use them to add textural interest in the foreground and watch the vines sprawl across the terrarium floor. Create textural interest and warmth in a bathroom with a platter of nerve plants, where they will thrive in a lower light setting and soak up the extra humidity. Find unique ways to keep humidity levels high for these divas by housing them in cloches, cookie jars and apothecary jars—take a moment to rummage through your kitchen and have fun hunting down your perfect glass container.

BASIC CARE

Light
Medium to bright indirect light. Does not tolerate direct sun.

Water
Water thoroughly when soil is almost dry, keeping soil moist at all times. Enjoys humidity—mist regularly.

Substrate
Well-draining, tropical mix (page 51).

Nutrients
Water-soluble as new growth appears.

Common Problem
If an otherwise healthy *Fittonia* has recently been showing signs of yellowing leaves, it may be overwatered. Making sure the roots have not rotted, the plant may be salvaged by repotting in fresh soil and extending the time between watering. The nerve plant will let you know when it is thirsty by wilting dramatically—observe how long it takes for this occurrence and subtract a few days from this number to determine an ideal schedule.

FUN FACT
The *Fittonia* plant was named after botanist sisters Sarah and Elizabeth Fitton who influenced the popularity of botany as a field of scientific study for women in the 1800s.

Size + Growth Habit: upwards of 10 feet (3 m) tall + tree-like or clumping
Toxicity Level: Areca, Parlor, Ponytail are nontoxic; Sago is highly toxic

PALMS

There are no houseplants quite like that of the palm category to exude feelings of the balmy tropics. Cultivated in a range of sizes, these elegant indoor trees are prized for their large, feather-like pinnate leaves or fronds emerging from the top of an unbranched stem. While you may think that this stately group can only be grown in high light and humid environments, there are a good selection that will thrive in average household conditions, giving plant parents in all temperate regions the ability to create their own tropical oasis.

1. Sago
2. Areca
3. Ponytail
4. Parlor

HOW TO STYLE

A towering regal palm makes a stunning statement on its own, so simplicity is key to using them to style a space. Because they tolerate a wide spectrum of lighting situations, they can be placed in many parts of the home. Introduce an areca palm into a bright corner of a living room, den or lounge area to instantly transform the space into a relaxing retreat. Create a spa-like atmosphere with a calming parlor palm placed beside the bathtub and soak your troubles away. If space is an issue or you prefer a smaller plant, the sago palm or ponytail palm are two unique and whimsical alternatives to the traditional palm tree and can be placed as a tabletop piece. Take your time in selecting the planter as both of these plants are slow-growing and will not outgrow their pots for a while.

BASIC CARE

Light
Medium to bright indirect or dappled light, tolerating a few hours of direct sun each day. Low light tolerable.

Water
Water thoroughly when soil is almost dry to dry. Tolerates occasional drought. Enjoys humidity. Susceptible to fluoridated water, use distilled water with added nutrients, aquarium water or rainwater.

Substrate
Tropical mix (page 51) with added sand or cactus mix (page 51).

Nutrients
Slow-release, water-soluble as new growth appears.

Common Problem
Dry, stagnant air can harbor pests like spider mites. Quarantine the plant and spray with diluted alcohol in the shower or bathtub. Let the solution sit for about fifteen to twenty minutes and rinse thoroughly. Repeat about every seven to ten days or align treatment with watering days to avoid overwatering when rinsing it with the solution. Continue treatment until all signs of mites disappear completely, with a total of around two to four treatments until fully eradicated.

FUN FACT
In addition to growing dates and coconuts, palms can be used to create palm wine, a sweet alcoholic beverage popular across Asia and Africa.

Size + Growth Habit: upwards of 3 feet (1 m) tall + upright
Toxicity Level: mildly toxic when ingested

PEACE LILIES
Spathiphyllum

1

2

3

Attract positive energy in your home with a beautiful peace lily. The lush green foliage and hardy nature of the peace lily make it one of the most popular and readily available plants out there. A peace lily will diligently purify the air, neutralizing toxins like formaldehyde and carbon monoxide and will also let you know when it requires a drink with its tell-tale leaf droop. Give it enough light and this plant will reward you with simple white blooms in the spring throughout the fall. Pruning spent flowers at the base will encourage better growth and encourage more blooms.

1. Mauna Loa
2. Domino
3. Little Angel

HOW TO STYLE

Display a peace lily almost anywhere in the home. Reset your mind and give your eyes a break from the screen by placing one in the office space. For a spa-like retreat, situate one or even several in a small bathroom. For larger spaces, create textural interest by combining a peace lily with other humidity-loving foliage like ferns (page 105) and another lower light forgiving plant like a ZZ plant (page 165), creating hierarchy by placing the tallest and fullest plants in the back and the shortest and smallest—or those with trailing habits—in the foreground. Use neutral, subdued tones and even natural materials when it comes to choosing decorative planters to complement the tranquil, pure and relaxed style of the peace lily.

BASIC CARE

Light
Medium to bright indirect or dappled light. Low light tolerable.

Water
Water thoroughly when soil is almost dry to dry or at the first sign of leaf droop, being sure not to wait too long after this occurs. Enjoys humidity.

Substrate
Well-draining, chunky mix.

Nutrients
Sensitive to chemical fertilizers. Organic is best to avoid salt buildup which will result in browning tips of the leaves.

Common Problem
Brown leaf tip commonly occurs in peace lilies and can be caused by either over-watering or underwatering. Overwater the plant and the minerals present in the soil cause water to start to accumulate and burn the tips. If the plant experiences drought too often, expect the tips to start drying out as a result. Strike a balance when it comes to watering by observing the number of days before the peace lily wilts and water thoroughly a day or two before this happens. Peace lilies are also sensitive to fluoride present in tap water, also a culprit of browning tips—use distilled water, fish tank water or rainwater.

FUN FACT
Peace lilies got their name from European explorers who thought the white flowers looked like white flags, a symbol of truce.

PHILODENDRONS

Philodendron

With almost 500 known species of the beloved philodendron, there are always new and emerging varieties and cultivars to enter the houseplant market. Available in two types of growth habits, upright and vining, with a plethora of color variations, textures, shapes and sizes, it is hard to believe that some are from the same genus. Adaptable and tolerant of varying conditions with growing requirements similar to pothos (page 141), which philodendrons are often mistaken with, both are versatile entry-level plants with unique differences to note.

1. Red Emerald
2. Congo Green
3. Birkin
4. Mayoi
5. Brasil
6. Micans
7. Heart Leaf
8. Silver Sword

HOW TO STYLE

Because the philodendron genus is so diverse, you can find species to suit every design purpose or situation. Do you have a large space for a statement piece and want to inject some jungle vibes? Create emphasis with a colossal philodendron Congo. Do you want a unique variegated plant with a designer look without the designer price tag? Pair a striking pinstriped philodendron birkin with a modern gold or marble planter. Do you want to create vertical movement in a room but don't want to hang a plant off the ceiling? Situate a towering showpiece with a stately philodendron red emerald totem—a potted plant, usually vining, that has been affixed to a stake or moss pole by the nursery. Do you love all the trailing plants so much, you want them to be the first things you see waking up? Combine all of your favorite trailers and make a dreamy, draped headboard above your bed. Sweet dreams!

BASIC CARE

Light
Medium to bright indirect or dappled light, tolerating a few hours of direct sun each day. Low light tolerable.

Water
Water thoroughly when soil is almost dry to dry. Tolerates occasional drought. Enjoys humidity.

Substrate
Well-draining, chunky mix.

Nutrients
Slow-release, water-soluble as new growth appears.

Common Problem
May suffer from mealybugs and spider mites. Spot treat small infestations of mealy bugs—individual insects, or clusters typically found in crevices; read more on page 64—with a cotton swab and alcohol. For more serious infestations and larger plants, quarantine them away from other plants and treat with my Homemade Insecticidal Soap Spray (page 66).

FUN FACT
The heart-shaped philodendron earns its name from two Greek words: *philo* or "loving" and *dendron* meaning "tree."

Size + Growth Habit: upwards of 10 feet (3 m) or longer + vining
Toxicity Level: mildly toxic when ingested

POTHOS
Epipremnum

No beginner's plant collection is complete without at least one or more species of the faithful and widely available pothos. With so many cultivars to choose from, there is a style to impress each and every new plant parent. This versatile and easy maintenance classic will bring life to any spot in the home or office, all the while filtering out toxins like formaldehyde from the air. With an impressive rate of feedback, you can expect to easily propagate cuttings to grow more plants, gift them to friends and family, replant them back into the main pot for a fuller look or leave the vines unpruned and let them grow wild.

1. Golden
2. Marble Queen
3. Snow Queen
4. Pearls and Jade
5. N'Joy
6. Neon
7. Jade
8. Cebu Blue

HOW TO STYLE

You can't go wrong when it comes to styling with the versatile and affordable pothos. For simplicity, place a larger specimen up high, cascading down the crown of a kitchen cabinet to brighten up the entertaining area. Place several medium-sized pothos on a bookshelf, alternating sides on each tier to create movement. If space and light permits, arrange a pothos living wall by combining a menagerie of contrasting varieties using wall planters. As a rapidly growing houseplant, pothos can be propagated time and again, allowing you to pepper cuttings in glass jars throughout the home for pops of green in the powder room, kitchen counter, mantle, side tables and more.

BASIC CARE

Light
Medium to bright indirect or dappled light, tolerating a few hours of direct sun each day. Low light tolerable.

Water
Water thoroughly when soil is almost dry to dry. Tolerates occasional drought. Enjoys humidity.

Substrate
Well-draining, tropical mix (page 51).

Nutrients
Slow-release, water-soluble as new growth appears.

Common Problem
Not generally prone to pests but may suffer from scale or mealy bugs. Use cotton swabs dipped in alcohol to spot treat minor infestations. For more substantial infestations, my Homemade Insecticidal Soap Spray (page 66) can be used.

FUN FACT
In the wild, pothos are seen growing prolifically up tree trunks via aerial roots, covering any and all surfaces they can reach in order to get more light from above the canopy, thus their nickname, "Devil's Ivy."

RADIATOR PLANTS

Peperomia

A nontoxic, compact and whimsical genus of plants, radiator plants have exploded on the houseplant market. With well over 1,500 known species, you can throw a *Peperomia* party for a single genus and appreciate the variety it has to offer. They are available in an array of shapes, colors, textures and patterns—ones with watermelon stripes, others with tortoise shell spots, some crinkled or rippled, others mounding, upright or vining in growth habits. They can be propagated by leaf or stem cuttings or division. Due to these plants' scant root system, they do not need to be repotted often and actually appreciate being root-bound.

1. Watermelon
2. Hope
3. String of Turtles
4. Rosso
5. Rana Verde
6. Frost
7. Red Ripple
8. Picollo Banda
9. Raindrop

HOW TO STYLE

Due to the varied selection and availability of radiator plants, they make great specimens for all types of styling purposes. Choose smaller clumping varieties, or plants that tend to spread slowly in a cluster, to pair or group with other types of small tabletop plants like haworthias (page 113), nerve plants (page 125) or a juvenile string of hearts (page 161) with contrasting colors and textures, adding energy and interest to dining or breakfast tables, desks or side tables. Hang a quirky vining peperomia hope in the kitchen to boost your mood while you start your day or a cute little trailing string of turtles in the nursery room to create texture and rhythm to a wall shelf. Use repetition of smaller to medium-sized peperomia specimens to create unity and textural interest throughout a shelf. To help highlight and contrast plants in their containers, pair plants with solid-colored leaves with patterned planters and plants with texture or variegated varieties with solid ones.

BASIC CARE

Light
Medium to bright indirect. Low light tolerable. Do not expose to direct sunlight. Rotate often to create even growth.

Water
Water thoroughly when soil is almost dry to dry. Tolerates occasional drought. Enjoys humidity.

Substrate
Well-draining, tropical mix (page 51) or cactus mix (page 51).

Nutrients
Slow-release, water-soluble as new growth appears.

Common Problem
Wilting and leaf drop may occur as a result of overwatering or underwatering. If the soil appears to be waterlogged for long periods of time after initial watering, check the root system for signs of rot like darkened mushy roots—read more on page 68. You can try to salvage the plant by repotting it in fresh soil and waiting for about a week before watering again, followed by reducing watering frequency based on the initial schedule. If the root ball appears to be dry or compacted even after watering, you can try to bottom water by allowing your pot to sit in a tray of water only until the ball is fully saturated. Remove the plant immediately once this occurs or you risk overwatering your plant.

FUN FACT
This species is from the same family as the peppercorn plant *(Piper nigrum)* and is nicknamed the radiator plant due to its appreciation for warm air.

MR. SILLY

Size + Growth Habit: upwards of 3 feet (1 m) tall + climbing or trailing
Toxicity Level: mildly toxic when ingested

SATIN POTHOS
Scindapsus

Despite some of the common names for this plant, satin pothos is not a pothos (page 141) or philodendron (page 137) at all, but has adopted the name over the centuries due to the similarities and climbing habit of its close relatives. As a striking vining tropical, the forgiving satin pothos is prized for its silvery-gray splotches painted against velvety dark green cordate leaves. Tolerant of varying light levels, this stunner trails beautifully in a hanging basket or if placed in a humid environment, will latch and shingle up a moss pole. When thirsty, the leaves will curl slightly, letting you know it's time for a drink. Give these plants regular trims whenever they appear leggy. Over time, this technique will help produce a fuller plant. Alternatively, share this beauty with friends and family with the gift of cuttings (see page 82).

1. Silver Lady
2. Exotica
3. Moonlight
4. Silvery Ann
5. Argyraeus

HOW TO STYLE

For simplicity, a single large satin pothos specimen hung in an airy open space will shine on its own with its unique mottled leaves. In a grouping, pair a smaller satin pothos with other glaucous plants, like watermelon peperomia (page 145) and cebu blue pothos (page 141) to achieve textural interest while highlighting the distinct pale blue-green shades of these plants. Often seen trailing, situate satin pothos baskets on office, kitchen or living room shelves and watch its glamorous tendrils grow. If shelving space is unavailable, try propping this vining plant on a stool or trailing down the side of a side table or counter-top. They work well as focal point plants when placed among other houseplants.

BASIC CARE

Light
Low to bright indirect or dappled light, tolerating a few hours of direct sun each day.

Water
Water thoroughly when soil is almost dry to dry. Tolerates occasional drought. Enjoys humidity.

Substrate
Well-draining, tropical mix (page 51).

Nutrients
Slow-release, water-soluble, all-purpose as new growth appears.

Common Problem
The satin pothos is generally free of pest problems. More often than not, the most common issue is an extended period of leaf curl, even after watering. If watering has been ruled out, try moving the plant to a brighter spot in the house, free from direct sunlight and watering once the soil has dried out.

FUN FACT
The botanical name *Scindapsus pictus* is derived from the Greek words: *skindapsos*, meaning "upon tree trunks," while *pictus* means "painted," describing the leaves that are blistered with silver variegation.

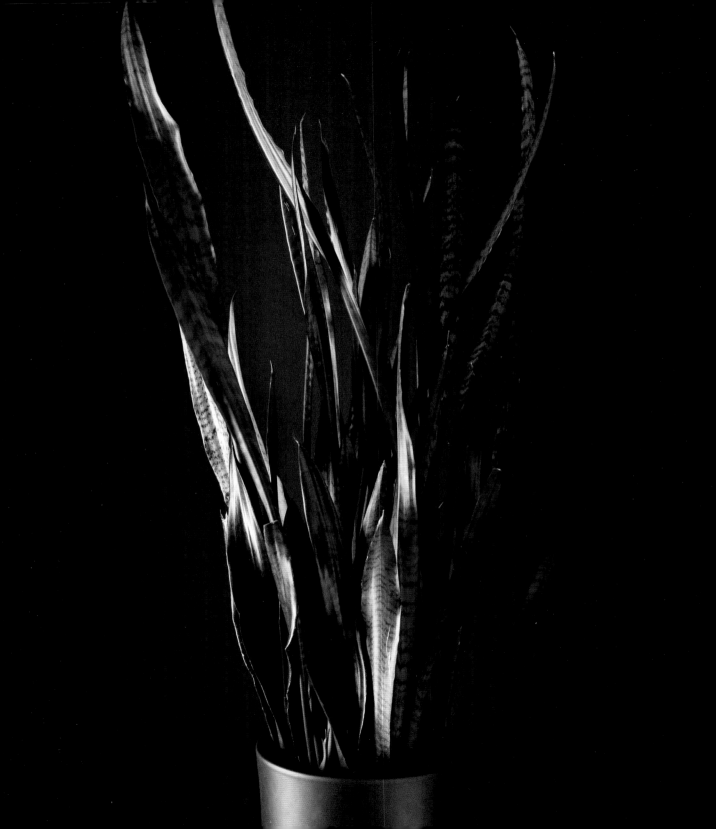

Size + Growth Habit: upwards of 4 feet (1 m) tall + upright
Toxicity Level: mildly toxic when ingested

SNAKE PLANTS
Dracaena

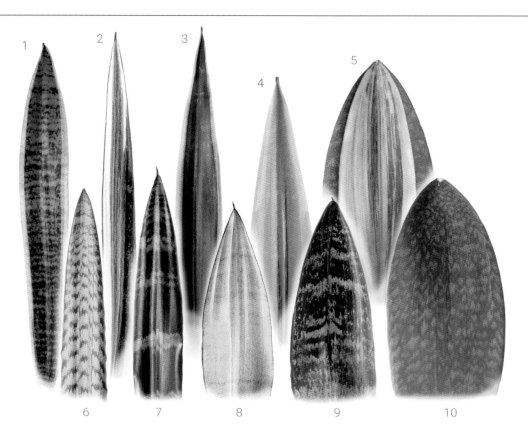

Snake plants are a slower-growing succulent with pointed, blade-like thick leaves, typically marked with wavy horizontal bands. With its upward growth habit, these tall and bold-looking plants lend themselves to tighter spaces, adding a graphic accent piece to almost any corner of the home with varying light levels. Tolerant of drier household conditions and able to withstand periods of drought, they are truly a die-hard houseplant that will thrive on neglect. With so many varieties of shapes, sizes and shades of green, there's a snake plant for every plant parent.

1. Laurentii
2. Bantel's Sensation
3. Black Gold
4. Gold Flame
5. Variegated Whale Fin
6. Zeylanica
7. Black Coral
8. Moonshine
9. Robusta
10. Whale Fin

HOW TO STYLE

The strikingly tall and slender shape of snake plants is forgiving in a space and helps to liven up any corner without demanding lateral growing room or particular light needs. If space permits, create a modern and clean snake nook, or "snook," by grouping several varieties of snake plants of varying heights in the same shade or color family of planters. Accentuate a tall snake for extra impact by placing the planter on a simple wooden stand. For an organic, air purifying and calming effect, transform multiple snake plants placed side by side into a room separator or privacy screen or even a funky headboard to help you sleep better at night!

BASIC CARE

Light
Low to bright indirect light, avoiding direct sun for long periods. Although snake plants can tolerate lower lighting, note that they will grow at a much slower rate. They are known to occasionally flower if given enough bright light.

Water
Water thoroughly when soil is completely dry, about once every three to four weeks. These troopers tolerate drought well—especially in the instance where light may be limited, so adjust your watering frequency accordingly.

Substrate
Snake plants are not fussy when it comes to potting medium, as long as water has the ability to drain freely through the bottom. Use a cactus mix (page 51) or regular potting soil amended with perlite and coconut husk.

Nutrients
Snake plants do not need fertilizer but will grow faster if given extra nutrients. Use an all-purpose plant food, slow-release, worm castings or similar soil enhancer.

Common Problem
Root rot due to overwatering is marked by soft, mushy, browning leaves that lift from the base of the plant fairly easily. Inspect the roots to see if they are still intact and not rotted away. Unfortunately, there is little you can do once the roots have died off. If some roots are still intact, remove as much of the damaged parts of the plant as possible and repot in fresh cactus mix (page 51). Resume watering in a few weeks and adjust your watering schedule by cutting back a week.

FUN FACT
Snake plants were originally under the *Sansevieria* genus, but in 2017 new DNA was discovered in the plant that caused it to be reclassified to the *Dracaena* genus.

Size + Growth Habit: upwards of 2 feet (1 m) wide + clumping
Toxicity Level: nontoxic

SPIDER PLANTS
Chlorophytum comosum

Widely available and a cinch to propagate, the nostalgic spider plant is every mom and grandma's favorite plant and for good reason. This highly adaptable and nontoxic staple injects bursts of greens into any room, while working hard to remove formaldehyde, carbon monoxide and other toxins in the air. When given plenty of light, a mature specimen will reward you with little "spiderettes" forming at the ends of long stems. These offshoots can be rooted easily in water and transplanted into soil (see page 81), instantly growing your plant collection or creating an opportunity to gift them to friends and family.

1. Variegated
2. Bonnie
3. Reverse Variegated
4. Green

HOW TO STYLE

Pair a small- to medium-sized spider plant with a simple, solid-colored, matte planter to elevate the look of this retro houseplant. Give this plant a fresh new vibe and pair with a mid-century modern plant hanger—think hangers with wood, gold or iron accents. Group a collection of spider plants in varying sizes and varieties to create harmony and textural movement in your kitchen. Hang a single large specimen in the bathroom to add warmth without worrying about the presence of lower light levels. In powder rooms, or where space is limited, display rooting offsets in glass bottles. Upcycle cosmetic vials, shot glasses, pickling jars or even champagne flutes for a pop of color and watch the robust roots flourish. These make affordable wedding and party favors as well. Make a spider bouquet by combining three varieties for a unique hostess gift.

BASIC CARE

Light
Medium to bright indirect or dappled light. Low light tolerable.

Water
Water thoroughly when soil is almost dry to dry. Enjoys humidity.

Substrate
Well-draining, tropical mix (page 51).

Nutrients
Organic fertilizer.

Common Problem
Browning tips are commonly seen in spider plants. If this occurs shortly after bringing home the plant, it may be stressed from drastic changes in climate—a drop in humidity can cause drying leaves. Mist often to prevent further damage. Your tap water may contain minerals and fluoride which can start to build up in the soil and show signs of burn at the tips. Use filtered, rain or fish tank water to alleviate the problem. At the very least, use tap water that has sat overnight.

FUN FACT
The *Chlorophytum comosum* "green" variety is potentially the original spider plant. Although better adapted to darker light than the variegated versions, it is surprisingly the least common variety found on the market today.

Size + Growth Habit: upwards of 3 feet (1 m) long + trailing

Toxicity Level: nontoxic

STRING OF HEARTS
Ceropegia

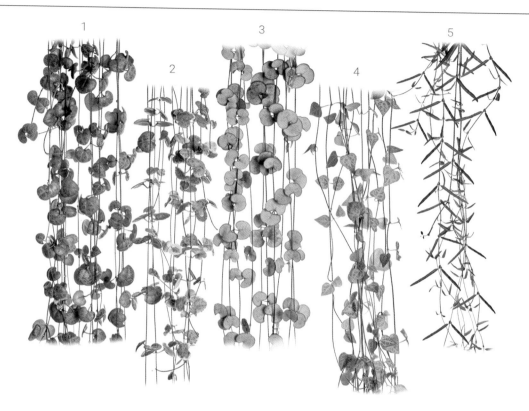

Pulling at your heartstrings is the charming vining semi-succulent, the string of hearts. These can be seen gracing the shelves and suspended from the ceilings of almost every plant lover's home, and justly so due to their forgiving nature and constant feedback. Care for this plant like you would succulents—a missed watering here and there won't phase it. Give it enough light and you'll be rewarded with intriguing little tubular purple-pink flowers. Along the vine, potato-like tubers called bulbils will form and can be propagated by inserting cuttings into water or soil to produce more plants—see page 82. The delicate yet hardy string of hearts will surely win your love and the hearts of others by sharing cuttings with friends and family.

1. Green
2. Variegated
3. Silver Glory
4. Spades
5. Needles

HOW TO STYLE

Due to the string of heart's svelte silhouette, this plant can be inserted into smaller, discreet nooks of the home without worrying that it will need to be relocated or overtake a space as it matures. Add textural interest to any north, east or west windowsill with a small specimen and watch the vines start to grow and spill over the edges. A mantle provides a secure placement for adding several varieties of strings, out of curious little hands and paws' reach. Create rhythm on a wall of floating shelves or narrow picture ledges by staggering strings that lead the viewer from tier to tier. For simplicity, style a larger specimen in a basket on its own, hung from the ceiling or draping from a staircase ledge, and let its understated and easy-care qualities thrive.

BASIC CARE

Light
Medium to bright indirect or dappled light, tolerating a few hours of direct sun each day. Enjoys bright light, resulting in purple-hued leaf undersides and purple-pink flowers.

Water
Water thoroughly when soil is dry. Tolerates occasional drought. Enjoys humidity.

Substrate
Well-draining cactus mix (page 51).

Nutrients
Does not require fertilizer to be happy. However, a liquid cacti fertilizer or mild soil enhancers like worm castings can be used during active growth.

Common Problem
String of hearts are not typically prone to pests. However, if the leaves are curling, or if more variegation is desired—it may be a sign there is not enough light—move to a brighter spot. Puckering or soft leaves indicate that it is time to water.

FUN FACT
As a string of hearts vine matures, the base below or just breaching the soil's surface will develop a caudex. This thickened stem or bulbous base acts as a water-storing system allowing the plant to withstand periods of drought.

Size + Growth Habit: upwards of 3 feet (1 m) tall + upright
Toxicity Level: mildly toxic when ingested

ZZ PLANTS
Zamioculcas zamiifolia

A slower-growing loyal soldier tolerant of many conditions, the ZZ plant has become a household hero prized for its ability to thrive even through repeated neglect. This hardy upright growing succulent with its deep green, thick and waxy leaves can brighten up any room. It has varied need for light levels and will not fuss if you miss a watering. This carefree houseplant is also known to improve air quality by removing harmful toxins including benzene, toluene and xylene, which are found in household chemicals. Because of their slower growth rate, you do not need to worry about giving them a bigger space to grow into, saving time and effort on repotting duties.

1. Green
2. Raven
3. Zenzi

HOW TO STYLE

The stalwart ZZ plant can instantly transform a space into a charming retreat with its east African Zanzibar origins where it was originally discovered. Since it is not particular to any special lighting or watering requirements, place this specimen in any space that needs life and a bit of glitz, instantly brightening up a shadier corner with their glossy, almost artificial-looking deep green pinnate leaves. Pair a ZZ plant with a simple solid matte white planter to create chic contrast. For a casual, traditional African look, combine a ZZ with natural woven textures made from organic materials such as grasses, sisal or raffia.

BASIC CARE

Light
Low to bright indirect light, tolerating a few hours of direct sun each day.

Water
Water thoroughly when soil is completely dried out. Tolerates occasional drought.

Substrate
Any well-draining potting mix will do, though a cactus mix (page 51) is recommended.

Nutrients
Does not need fertilizer to thrive, but a slow-release or balanced fertilizer during active growth will speed growth.

Common Problem
Often times, droopy fronds can result from a lack of light, or growth towards one light source. In this case, move the plant to a brighter spot, but always rotate every month or so for even growth.

FUN FACT
Although the ZZ plant was botanically discovered in the 1800s, large-scale cultivation and distribution was only recently started in 1996 by Dutch nurseries.

CREATE

What better way to direct the creative energy plants can promote than to build something for them! The shelving projects in this chapter vary in look, complexity, size and purpose and use materials that you can find at your local hardware store or conveniently online.

Elevate the look of your favorite trailing beauties with a suspended tray decked out in boating hardware, featuring mold-resistant rope (page 170). For the ultimate curated living wall, customize your very own #melsshelfie (page 178) for those small to medium-sized plants of varying sizes and growth habits.

These unique and practical installations are a result of my growing plant collection where I needed space-saving solutions to display and keep my jungle from disarray. Put your green friends on a pedestal—or shelf, rather—with these step-by-step builds.

DECKED UP SUSPENDED TRAY

Bring a little nautical vibe into the home with this unique, contemporary suspended tray to display your favorite vining green babies. Featuring brass boating hardware and durable hemp-like rope made exclusively to withstand rot, this décor piece can be customized for various practical and aesthetic applications around the home. Save space by suspending multiple trays up high or position one lower to the ground to be used as a side table beside your bed or lounge chair. Let your plants cascade down the edges of the tray or wrap them around the main rope to train your vines to grow skyward. The contrast between wood, rope and glitz is the perfect complement to the green foliage of your plants. These instructions will make an approximately 3½-foot (1-m) long hanging tray mounted to ceiling joists.

MATERIALS

1 (1-inch [2.5-cm]) brass hook +
end plate (see Building Tips)

4 (#8x2 inch [#8x5 cm])
construction screws

1 (1-inch [2.5-cm]) brass cup
end (see Building Tips)

3 #6 (⅜-inch [1-cm]) brass
screws

2 feet (0.5 m) Hempex® rope,
1-inch (25-mm) thick

3 (½-inch [1.3-cm]) brass eye
bolts

1 wooden tray, 15 inches
(38 cm) in diameter

1 (42-inch [1-m]) brass
plumber's chain

3 #6 brass flat washers

3 #6 brass hex nuts

Toggle bolts (optional;
see Building Tips)

TOOLS

Stud finder

Pencil (optional)

Screwdriver

Power drill + drill bit $^9/_{64}$ inch
(3.66 mm)

Lighter

Pliers

Wire cutter

Utility knife (optional)

BUILDING TIPS

Your brass hook, end plate and cup end will all be sold with their own screws. However, when mounting your end plate to the ceiling do not use the supplied mounting screws, as they are not suitable for ceiling fixtures.

Ceiling joists or beams are recommended for hanging objects off ceilings to ensure maximum support. If this is not at all possible, the next best option is the use of toggle bolts, especially for weight loads that are 10 pounds [4.5 kg] and above. Use your discretion to find the best option for your purposes.

STEPS

End Plate Installation

1. Locate the ceiling joist(s) using the stud finder (see Building Tips).

2. Mount the end plate to the ceiling with a screwdriver using the construction screws.

Hook + Cup Ends Installation

3. Seal the cut ends of the Hempex® rope by lightly running the ends under the flame of the lighter.

4. Insert one end of the rope fully into the brass hook hardware.

5. Using the $^9/_{64}$-inch (3.66-mm) drill bit, pre-drill a hole through the rope where the screw provided with your hook end hardware will be installed, paying close attention to the alignment to ensure the drill bit reaches the exit hole.

6. With a screwdriver, install the screw to fasten the hardware to the rope. This may require some elbow grease to align.

7. Repeat steps 3 through 6 with the brass cup end to secure the hardware to the other end of the rope and complete the rope extension.

8. Drill three pilot holes spaced evenly around into the lip of the tray.

9. Screw on the three brass eye bolts with pliers.

10. Using a wire cutter, cut the plumber's chain to make three equal lengths of 14-inch (36-cm) pieces of chain.

11. Using pliers, slightly bend open each of the eye bolts and loop each end of the three chains. Close the eye bolts.

12. To secure the loose end of the chain, insert the #6 screw through a hole of the end cap, followed by the chain, washer and hex nut. Repeat this step for the other loose ends.

13. Hook the top of the brass hook into the brass plate on the ceiling, arrange your vining plant babies as you see fit and stand back and admire your decked-up tray.

PROJECT TIPS

Take time to hunt down the perfect trays or platforms for your plants at home décor centers and department stores. Trays with a small lip are great for keeping pots and items contained. Sturdy trays with natural grain and wood construction are both great options aesthetically and for durability when drilling into or during use. Avoid flimsy options that may break or collapse under the weight of your pots.

When searching for hardware, opt for sturdy metals and construction that can hold up the weight of your tray. Avoid using delicate chains and fittings that can easily warp and bend over time.

If you purchased extra rope that requires cutting down, avoid fraying fibers and make clean cuts by taping around the rope where the cut will be made; scotch, duct and painter's tape will work in this case.

Some helpful websites to order materials from include Amazon, AliExpress, Etsy and Home Depot.

DESIGN TIPS

Think about how the piece will fit into the existing décor of your home—complement the wood tray with other wooden details or stain the wood to highlight specific color palettes of your home. Tuck multiple suspended pieces in the corner of a brightly lit room for vertical interest. For contrasting colors and textures, use a mix of glass, metal and ceramic planters of varying heights displayed on a single tray. Add a personal touch by including small trinkets and items of personal sentiment.

Experiment with various materials for the main rope extension, natural or synthetic—hemp, cotton, nylon and polypropylene among many others may be found at your local hardware or crafting store.

Keep the ratio between natural or natural-like materials and neutral colors high and only accent with synthetic or metallic details. Think plenty of wooden and stone finishes and natural fiber textiles, with pops of gold or chrome hardware. Look for organic lines when searching for décor—the natural curves and jagged edges of wood and stone complement the raw nature of these materials.

When choosing plants to display on this tray, consider vining plants that can be trained to climb up the rope for a different look. Use coated garden wire or garden tape to affix the vines to the rope.

#MELSSHELFIE

Design and build a five-tier living wall curated for your plant collection. This metal and wood construction display is staggered to suit the varying heights and growing habits of your plant collection. From small to large, trailing to upright and everything in between, this versatile shelf project is a unique space-saving solution to display your growing plant family. Mount this green shrine in your home to elevate tropical retreat vibes and immerse yourself in floor-to-ceiling greenery all seasons of the year.

MATERIALS

5 ($^5/_4$ x 6–inch [3.18 x 15.25–cm]) pieces lumber (see Building Tips)

Interior wood stain

Polyurethane seal

Drywall anchors + screws (see Building Tips)

10 (11 x 4¾–inch [30 x 12–cm]) IKEA GRANHULT brackets

Wood screws

TOOLS

Stud finder

Pencil

Painter's tape

Hand, table or circular saw (see Building Tips)

Sandpaper in 80-, 120- and 180-grit

Sanding block (optional)

Level

Drop cloth

Latex gloves

Clean cloths

Paint brush

Power drill

BUILDING TIPS

It is important to know that with most dimensional lumber, what is labeled and sold at stores may not reflect the true measurements of the finished product. Although lumber yards list materials to be $^5/_4$ x 6–inch (3.18 x 15.25–cm), they are in fact 1 x 5.25–inch (2.5 x 13.33–cm). For the #melsshelfie build, 2 pieces of lumber at this size are used to fit the depth of the 11-inch (28-cm) brackets (see photo on page 183).

Identify the type of wall you're working with and use appropriate wall anchors. Securing the shelves to studs is recommended whenever possible as this offers greater support compared to drywall anchors. It is important to take note of the combined weight of plants and objects placed on each tier, so select anchors that support the load of your shelves. Recommended drywall anchors: E-Z Ancor® Twist-N-Lock #8.

Skip at-home cutting by getting the lumber cut at the hardware store. Call ahead to ask if they have a complimentary cutting service—the number of cuts will vary depending on the store and some will charge a small fee for subsequent cuts.

STEPS

Prep

1. Locate the studs using a stud finder and mark them on the wall with small pieces of painter's tape. These will be used as reference points to determine the types of screws and fixings needed when it comes time to mount the shelves and put in the brackets.

2. Mock the shelves on your wall in their entirety using strips of painter's tape. This serves as a visual aid for the overall design, ensuring adjustments can be easily made.

For reference, #melsshelfie was built on an approximately 6 x 9–foot (2 x 3–m) wall using a combination of wood screws through studs and drywall anchors for maximum support. The following numbers are the predetermined shelving lengths that I found best suit my plants and design sense.

#melsshelfie Lengths	
1st (top tier)	28" (71 cm)
2nd	36" (91 cm)
3rd	42" (106 cm)
4th	40" (101 cm)
5th (bottom tier)	28" (71 cm)

Distance between shelves: 13 inches (33 cm).

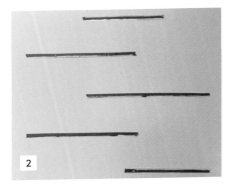

Wood Tiers

3. Cut the lumber to appropriate lengths based on your mock-up.

4. Thoroughly sand all surfaces and edges first with the 80-grit sandpaper to remove any imperfections in the wood. You can also use a sanding block for this step, if desired. Wipe off the dust. Follow with the 120-grit sandpaper and sand until the surface appears level. Again, wipe off the dust. Finish with the 180-grit sand-paper to remove any residual marks left by the 120-grit paper. Wipe clean.

5. Stain the wood panels, working over a drop cloth and in a well-ventilated area. Latex gloves will help with messes. Thoroughly stir the stain before applying. When applying stain, the cloth you apply it with should be wet but not dripping. Work a thin coat of product evenly onto all sides and edges of the panels. Immediately following a coat of stain, use a clean cloth to wipe any excess product. Let the panels dry thoroughly. If you want a deeper color, repeat this step.

6. Using a clean paint brush, apply one or two thin coats of the polyurethane sealer. This will help protect the surfaces from moisture, scratches and fading. Let the panels dry and cure completely for approximately 24 hours.

Installation

7. Level and drill the first bracket directly into the wall using wood screws if you are mounting to a stud. On the other hand, if you are using anchors, first level the bracket and use a pencil to mark the drill holes on the wall, setting aside the bracket.

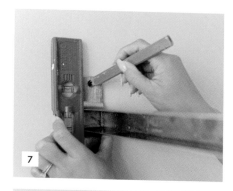

8. Screw in the drywall anchors where the drill holes were marked.

9. Mount the bracket by screwing the screws into the anchors using a power drill.

10. Insert the appropriate finished panels into the mounted bracket.

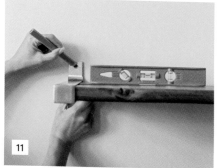

11. Attach the second bracket on the opposite side with the level placed on top of the panel and repeat step 7. Proceed with steps 8 and 9 if you are mounting the bracket to drywall.

12. Repeat steps 7 through 11 for the remainder of the finished panels.

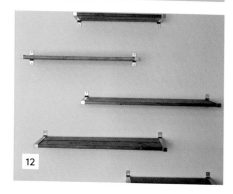

AFTERCARE

Wipe down the shelves of dust and debris to keep the panels looking new. Sand, re-stain and reseal as needed from wear and tear. Avoid letting water pool on the panels for long periods by wiping down excess moisture during watering and using drip-trays and saucers whenever possible.

PROJECT TIPS

Locate a clean wall in your home to build your wall display. A brightly lit and warm area free from extreme temperature fluctuations and drafts is an ideal environment for thriving houseplants. A wall with plenty of window light shining into a south-, east- or west-facing room are great options for plants of varying light requirements. Note that plants grow towards a light source, so rotate your green babies every so often for even growth. See page 23 for more about light.

If sanding, staining and sourcing your own wood panels is not your forte, forgo this process by conveniently purchasing complementing IKEA BERGSHULT shelves. Note that the color options are limited and the panels are constructed of particleboard and synthetic finishes.

Of the various wood stains, the oil-based type tends to seep into the wood pores without raising the grain. Water-based wood stain tends to stain more evenly and be more environmentally friendly. Gel-based stains are thicker, allowing better control of color. Gel-based stains work well with pine to prevent the blotchiness that oil or water-based stains might cause.

Speak to your local hardware store or paint specialist for appropriate conditioners or fillers for certain wood types that may need to be applied before staining. Cut up old T-shirts to make stain cloths. Always read and follow instructions on product labels since this can vary from one product to another.

DESIGN TIPS

Survey your plant collection to determine which specimens have unique spacing requirements and can be thought of as the feature plants. A juvenile snake plant (page 153) with upright growing blades will eventually need overhead clearance in the next several years. A vining pothos (page 141) will cascade as it matures, so a position up high will allow it to grow into its vertical space.

With various bracket types and styles to choose from, you can explore different materials, colors and finishes to suit your personality and style sense. Shop online in the comforts of your home or take a walk around your local home improvement store, home décor center or anywhere home accessories are sold for the perfect shelfie brackets.

Add a personal touch by expressing other hobbies and interests on your display. Place little trinkets and souvenirs from travels, items of personal sentiment or gifts from loved ones alongside your plant babies to create a vignette of love, growth and individual narrative—a curated composition that instills a moment of awareness, sense of calm and promotes reflection.

ACKNOWLEDGMENTS

Thankfully growing together with . . .

Justin
A special thank you to my husband and partner-in-crime. You brought life to this book in unimaginable ways and transformed the ordinary into the extraordinary with your stunning art and meticulous attention to detail. I love you for your brilliant mind, your intense passion in all that you set your heart to and your brute humor. You are the architect and mastermind behind #melsshelfie where my passion for plants grew and the journey continues with your enduring support and commitment. Love grows every day alongside our children in our ever-evolving home we continue to build together, our oasis.

Family + Friends
Thank you to my family for their unconditional love, support and free babysitting services that have allowed me the time to complete this book. To my newly acquired and childhood friends and colleagues who have shared a plant moment with me one time or another, my "designerd A.M." girls, friends and neighbors of the Cornell Community: Thank you for your counsel and immense support, inspiring me throughout this ongoing houseplant journey and putting the fate of your plants in my hands.

Valleyview Gardens

Many thanks and gratitude to my number one plant dealer Valleyview Gardens together with Tanya Carvalho, Larry Varlese and the staff, all of whom are responsible for turning my home into a jungle and a green oasis for my family, our guests and the world to marvel over. Thank you for the generous support, giving life to *Houseplant Oasis* and for fulfilling so many of my houseplant dreams and wish lists.

Page Street Publishing Team

Thank you to the Page Street Publishing team for their commitment, expertise and professionalism throughout the creation of this labor of love. Thank you for reaching out at the most opportune time and placing your faith in my knowledge, work and creative process. Working meticulously with Frances Donington and the Page Street Publishing team has been nothing short of a smooth and collaborative effort! Thank you for the transformative experience of turning my passion and vision into something tactile to be able to share with the world.

The Online Houseplant Community

A big shout-out to the crazy plant lovers and enablers of the online houseplant community. Together, we have shared the trials and tribulations of plant parenthood, successes, tips and tricks, peeves, hacks and wish lists and above all, to just "buy the damn plant!" You guys are my teachers and the reason this book exists, so thank you!

ABOUT THE AUTHOR

Melissa Lo is a Canadian designer and the creator of Instagram account @houseplant.oasis where she shares her passion for design, growth and life. She is a proud mother of two children and over one-hundred plants which she nurtures with care and compassion. Born and raised in Toronto, she gained a worldwide following for her unique style, inspirational designs and plant parenting advice through social media. This is her first book.

INDEX